JULIUS CAESAR

HBJ SHAKESPEARE

JULIUS CAESAR

edited by
Allan Patenaude

Harcourt Brace Jovanovich, Canada

Toronto Orlando San Diego London Sydney

HBJ Shakespeare: Series Editor, Ken Roy

Canadian Cataloguing in Publication Data

Shakespeare, William, 1564–1616
  Julius Caesar

(HBJ Shakespeare)
For use in high schools.
ISBN 0-7747-1261-9

I. Caesar, Julius – Drama.   I. Patenaude, Allan.
II. Title.   III. Series.

PR2808.P38 1987   822.3'3   C87-093767-7

88 89 90 91 92 5 4 3 2

Editorial Director: Murray Lamb
Senior Editor: Lydia Fletcher
Production Editor: Dick Hemingway
Designer: Michael van Elsen
Illustrators: Marika and Laszlo Gal
Cover Illustrators: Marika and Laszlo Gal
Typesetter: Q Composition
Printed in Canada by Friesen Printers

Acknowledgments

The editor and publisher acknowledge the consultants listed below for their contribution to the development of this program:

Leuba Bailey
English Teacher, Daniel McIntyre Collegiate, Winnipeg School Division, Winnipeg, Manitoba

Coralie Bryant
Language Arts Consultant, Secondary Schools, Winnipeg, Manitoba

To the Reader

The text of a play provides the material for creating drama on stage. The language of the text inspires directors, actors, designers, technicians, and audiences to create together their sense of the play. Through activities provided in this edition of *Julius Caesar*, you have many opportunities to participate in the process of creating your own sense of the play.

Before reading the scenes in this play, you will be invited to discuss thoughts and experiences similar to ones the characters will encounter. Following scenes and acts, you will have the opportunity to explore some of the ideas, themes, and feelings you experienced while reading the text, as you complete selected activities. Your personal responses and reactions to the scenes and acts will provide the starting points for working through the activities. Your first impressions are always important.

Some of the activities ask you to consider the text through the eyes of a director. Others invite you to see the play through an actor's or designer's eyes. Many encourage you to bring your own experiences to events and circumstances which, although they happened many centuries ago, have significance for today's audiences.

At times you may choose to work alone as you complete chosen activities. At other times you may wish to work with one or several partners. Frequently, you will need to return to the text as you develop and/or confirm initial responses to the scenes in which you are participating. In doing so, you will be using this edition of *Julius Caesar* in the way for which it is intended — as a springboard for creative involvement.

Getting Started

We live in a country where we enjoy the benefits of a political system that is democratic — government by the people for the people. Of course, this form of government is not found in every country in the world today, nor has it always been the system of rule throughout history. One focus of *Julius Caesar* is that of government and its leadership. Some of the questions that audiences are encouraged to consider are the following:

- What constitutes leadership?
- What qualifies a person to seek or assume leadership?
- How should leadership be attained and maintained?
- What should be the relationship between the leadership of a government and the people it governs?

All of these questions arise in the development of this play. The play has other main ideas, however, such as friendship, partnership, superstition, jealousy, fear, ambition, social order and revolution, power, and citizenship. All of these are familiar to us because we too are a part of the same humanity that William Shakespeare wrote about in his plays.

Before you explore the drama of *Julius Caesar*, you may wish to discuss some of the questions and themes presented in this play. This will give you a good opportunity to begin writing in your journal. Record what you think are some of the important and interesting points that were made in your discussions. These thoughts and opinions will become reference points for you as you select activities to complete following the various scenes and acts in this play. You might consider the following questions for discussion and for journal writing responses as well.

1. What are the five most important qualities a political leader of a country needs? Why is it necessary for him or her to possess each of these?

2. In Canada, what provisions exist for the political opponents of the party in power to express themselves?

3. Many countries in the world are suffering or have suffered from social and political unrest. Choose one of these countries and situations you know about to discuss. Explain the causes and events of the political unrest to your group. If you were the country's political leader, what might you do to quell the unrest?

4. Think of a contemporary or historical person who has dedicated his or her life to a cause.
   - What difficulties did he or she encounter while promoting the cause?
   - What were the results of his or her efforts?
   - Did the person experience any failures in representing the cause? If so, how did he or she handle them?
   - What successes did the person achieve?

Talk about your ideas. If necessary, do some research to support your information.

5. *Julius Caesar* is set in early Roman times. The society of that time was in many ways an advanced one. With the assistance of your teacher and/or librarian, research some of the influences that Roman society has had on our modern world. Share your findings with other members of your group.

6. What characteristics do you associate with "ambitious" people? Describe the qualities that an ambitious person you know possesses. Are you attracted to the person? Why or why not?

7. How do you think modern political leaders in Canada make their government-related decisions? Who are some of the people they might consult? If you were leader of a Canadian political party, whose counsel would you seek before making a decision that might affect the social and economic welfare of the people?

Dramatis Personae

(Characters in the Play)

Julius Cæsar
Octavius Cæsar ⎰ triumvirs
Marcus Antonius ⎱ after the death
M. Æmilius Lepidus of Julius Cæsar
Cicero
Publius ⎱ senators
Popilius Lena
Marcus Brutus
Cassius
Casca
Trebonius conspirators
Ligarius against
Decius Brutus Julius Cæsar
Metellus Cimber
Cinna
Flavius and **Marullus,** tribunes
Artemidorus (of Cnidos), a teacher of rhetoric
A Soothsayer
Cinna, a poet. Another Poet
Lucilius
Titinius
Messala friends to Brutus
Young Cato and Cassius
Volumnius
Varro
Clitus
Claudius
Strato servants to Brutus
Lucius
Dardanius
Pindarus, servant to Cassius
Calpurnia, wife to Cæsar
Portia, wife to Brutus
Senators, Citizens, Attendants, etc.
Scene: Rome; the neighbourhood of Sardis; the neighbourhood
of Philippi.

Act 1, Scene 1

In this scene . . .

A group of working class citizens who have taken a holiday to celebrate the triumphal procession of Caesar are approached by two tribunes, Flavius and Marullus. The tribunes, who are officers of Rome appointed by the government to protect the rights of commoners, are annoyed to find the citizens taking a holiday from work to celebrate Caesar's victory in battle.

During the encounter between the tribunes and the citizens, we learn about the political climate of Rome in this year of 44 B.C. We also learn about the mood and behaviour of the Roman citizens, who become very important to the development of political events in later scenes.

3   *mechanical:* manual labourers, trades people

7   *rule:* ruler

10-11 *in respect of a fine workman:* in comparison with a skilled labourer

11   *cobbler:* shoemaker; also, a person who is inept at his or her work

16   *knave:* an unprincipled or crafty person

17   *be not out:* don't be angry

24   *awl:* a pointed tool used for making holes in leather

26   *trod upon neat's leather:* walked in leather shoes; *neat:* cattle

Act 1, Scene 1

Rome. A street.

*Enter Flavius, Marullus, and
certain Commoners.*

Flavius: Hence! Home, you idle creatures, get you home,
Is this a holiday? what! know you not,
Being mechanical, you ought not walk
Upon a labouring day without the sign
Of your profession? Speak, what trade art thou?   5
First Commoner: Why, sir, a carpenter.
Marullus: Where is thy leather apron and thy rule?
What dost thou with thy best apparel on?
You, sir, what trade are you?
Second Commoner: Truly, sir, in respect of a fine workman,   10
I am but, as you would say, a cobbler.
Marullus: But what trade art thou? answer me directly.
Second Commoner: A trade, sir, that, I hope, I may use with
a safe conscience; which is indeed, sir, a mender of
bad soles.   15
Marullus: What trade, thou knave? thou naughty knave,
what trade?
Second Commoner: Nay, I beseech you, sir, be not out with
me: yet, if you be out, sir, I can mend you.
Marullus: What meanest thou by that? mend me, thou saucy
fellow!
Second Commoner: Why, sir, cobble you.   20
Flavius: Thou art a cobbler, art thou?
Second Commoner: Truly, sir, all that I live by is with the
awl: I meddle with no tradesman's matters, nor women's
matters; but with awl. I am, indeed, sir, a surgeon to
old shoes; when they are in great danger, I recover   25
them. As proper men as ever trod upon neat's leather
have gone upon my handiwork.

32   *triumph:* Caesar's return from Spain after defeating Pompey's sons

34   *tributaries:* captives

38   *Pompey:* a former ruler in Rome whom Caesar defeated in 48 B.C. and who was murdered a year later

47   *replication:* echo

50   *cull out:* choose to make

55   *intermit:* hold back, delay

56   *light:* fall

61   *most exalted shores:* the highest level on the shore to which the water rises

62   *basest metal:* the poor quality of their characters or dispositions

66   *decked with ceremonies:* decorated with ornaments

Flavius: But wherefore art not in thy shop to-day?
   Why dost thou lead these men about the streets?
Second Commoner: Truly, sir, to wear out their shoes, to   30
   get myself into more work. But, indeed, sir, we make
   holiday to see Cæsar and to rejoice in his triumph.
Marullus: Wherefore rejoice? What conquest brings he home?
   What tributaries follow him to Rome,
   To grace in captive bonds his chariot-wheels?   35
   You blocks, you stones, you worse then senseless things!
   O you hard hearts, you cruel men of Rome,
   Knew you not Pompey? Many a time and oft
   Have you climb'd up to walls and battlements,
   To towers and windows, yea, to chimney-tops,   40
   Your infants in your arms, and there have sat
   The live-long day, with patient expectation,
   To see great Pompey pass the streets of Rome:
   And when you saw his chariot but appear,
   Have you not made an universal shout,   45
   That Tiber trembled underneath her banks,
   To hear the replication of your sounds
   Made in her concave shores?
   And do you now put on your best attire?
   And do you now cull out a holiday?   50
   And do you now strew flowers in his way
   That comes in triumph over Pompey's blood?
   Be gone!
   Run to your houses, fall upon your knees.
   Pray to the gods to intermit the plague   55
   That needs must light on this ingratitude.
Flavius: Go, go, good countrymen, and, for this fault,
   Assemble all the poor men of your sort;
   Draw them to Tiber banks, and weep your tears
   Into the channel, till the lowest stream   60
   Do kiss the most exalted shores of all.
                              [*Exeunt all the Commoners.*]
   See, whether their basest metal be not moved;
   They vanish tongue-tied in their guiltiness.
   Go you down that way towards the Capitol;
   This way will I: disrobe the images,   65
   If you do find them decked with ceremonies.

68   *Lupercal:* a festival held on February 15 in honour of Lupercus, who protected herds and flocks, to ensure the fertility of the animals in the spring

71   *the vulgar:* the common people

74   *pitch:* height

76   *servile:* slavish

Marullus: May we do so?
  You know it is the feast of Lupercal.
Flavius: It is no matter; let no images
  Be hung with Cæsar's trophies. I'll about,   70
  And drive away the vulgar from the streets:
  So do you too, where you perceive them thick.
  These growing feathers plucked from Cæsar's wing
  Will make him fly an ordinary pitch,
  Who else would soar above the view of men   75
  And keep us all in servile fearfulness.

                                              [*Exeunt.*]

Act 1, Scene 1: Activities

1. a) In your journal write your first impressions of the mood of the citizens and the two tribunes, explaining why you think the citizens are so happy while the tribunes are annoyed. Remember that a tribune was elected by the people to protect the rights of the people.

   In groups, share your ideas. After hearing what others say, decide if you want to make any additions or changes to your journal entry.

   b) Why do Flavius and Marullus disrobe (take down the decorations from) the statues? In groups, discuss acts of civil disobedience today to which you could compare their actions.

2. The dialogue between Marullus and the second Commoner includes many examples of the pun (an amusing use of a word or phrase that has two meanings). What are some of the puns used in the conversation? Who used them? What are some puns you have used and/or heard? Why do you think people use them? Why did the second Commoner use them?

   Make a collection of puns and include as many of them as possible in a dialogue you write between two of the citizens.

3. The speeches of Marullus and Flavius succeed in breaking up the crowd. If you were one of these citizens, how would you feel as you left? In your role as a citizen, explain to others in your group why you feel as you do. Compare your reactions with those of others in your group. What does the reaction from the citizens reveal about them?

4. Prepare for presentation the speech by Marullus that begins, "Wherefore rejoice?" (lines 33–56). Consider what effect you want the speech to create in your audience. When you are ready, recite the speech as it is written or in your own words to your group.

Listen to other versions of the speech by your classmates. How are the presentations similar to yours? How are they different? Decide what was most effective about each speech and share your ideas.

5. What information do you learn from this scene about Caesar's return to Rome? Research the historical events that occurred prior to his arrival. Present your discoveries to the class in an appropriate form such as a chart or an oral discussion.

6. Investigate the traditions and significance of the Roman feast of the Lupercal. Why do you think Caesar chose to return to Rome at this time? What does this tell you about Caesar?

   If you had been Caesar, would you have returned at this time? Discuss your ideas.

7. Record the information that you learned from this scene in your journal. Make a note of questions you have about what may happen that you hope will be answered during your reading of the play. Come back to these questions when you finish reading this act and supply answers wherever possible. Respond to the remaining questions when you have finished the play.

For the next scene . . .

Think of a situation in which you might have to choose between a loyal friend and a cause in which you sincerely believe. Discuss what you think your eventual choice would be. What consequences would you fear? Has anyone ever persuaded you to do something you later regretted? How did he or she convince you at the time?

Act 1, Scene 2

In this scene . . .

Caesar's triumphal procession arrives in pomp and pageantry and soon moves on to the celebrations of the Feast of Lupercal. Cassius and Brutus, however, remain behind. They enter into a long conversation about important personal and political matters that will direct the course of action for the rest of the play. Twice during their discussion we hear the crowds shouting and the trumpets blaring in the distance.

Later, Caesar and his followers return from the festivities. Speaking to Antony, Caesar expresses his innermost feelings about Cassius. As the procession departs, Brutus pulls at Casca's cloak and urges Casca to report what happened at the celebrations.

Casca's account of the events leads Brutus to promise Cassius that he will think further about the matters they discussed. Alone on stage, Cassius now reveals his feelings about Brutus and his plans for his next move.

4   *run his course:* Antony, a priest of one of the orders of Luperci, would participate in the holy race during the festival.

8-9   *The barren . . . sterile curse:* It was believed that women who could not bear children would become capable of pregnancy if touched by a runner during the race.

15   *press:* crowd

18   *Ides of March:* March 15

Scene 2

A public place.

Flourish. Enter Cæsar; Antony,
for the course; Calpurnia, Portia,
Decius, Cicero, Brutus, Cassius,
and Casca; a great crowd
following, among them a
Soothsayer.

Cæsar: Calpurnia!
Casca: Peace, ho! Cæsar speaks.
Cæsar: Calpurnia!
Calpurnia: Here, my lord.
Cæsar: Stand you directly in Antonius' way,
   When he doth run his course. Antonius!
Antony: Cæsar, my lord?   5
Cæsar: Forget not, in your speed, Antonius,
   To touch Calpurnia; for our elders say,
   The barren, touchéd in this holy chase,
   Shake off their sterile curse.
Antony: I shall remember:
   When Cæsar says "Do this," it is performed.   10
Cæsar: Set on; and leave no ceremony out.   *[Flourish.]*
Soothsayer: Cæsar!
Cæsar: Ha! who calls?
Casca: Bid every noise be still: peace yet again!
Cæsar: Who is it in the press that calls on me?   15
   I hear a tongue, shriller than all the music,
   Cry "Cæsar!" Speak; Cæsar is turn'd to hear.
Soothsayer: Beware the Ides of March.
Cæsar: What man is that?
Brutus: A soothsayer bids you beware the Ides of March.
Cæsar: Set him before me; let me see his face.   20
Casca: Fellow, come from the throng; look upon Cæsar.

28   *gamesome:* fond of games

35   *bear . . . hand:* treat strictly and coldly

39   *Merely:* entirely
40   *of some difference:* conflicting
41   *Conceptions . . . myself:* matters or ideas that concern me alone

45   *construe:* interpret

50   *cogitations:* thoughts

58   *shadow:* reflection

Cæsar: What say'st thou to me now? speak once again.
Soothsayer: Beware the Ides of March.
Cæsar: He is a dreamer; let us leave him: pass.
              [Sennet. Exeunt all but Brutus and Cassius.]
Cassius: Will you go see the order of the course?   25
Brutus: Not I.
Cassius: I pray you, do.
Brutus: I am not gamesome: I do lack some part
  Of that quick spirit that is in Antony.
  Let me not hinder, Cassius, your desires;   30
  I'll leave you.

Cassius: Brutus, I do observe you now of late:
  I have not from your eyes that gentleness
  And show of love as I was wont to have:
  You bear too stubborn and too strange a hand   35
  Over your friend that loves you.
Brutus: Cassius,
  Be not deceived: if I have veil'd my look,
  I turn the trouble of my countenance
  Merely upon myself. Vexed I am
  Of late with passions of some difference,   40
  Conceptions only proper to myself,
  Which give some soil perhaps to my behaviours;
  But let not therefore my good friends be grieved—
  Among which number, Cassius, be you one—
  Nor construe any further my neglect,   45
  Than that poor Brutus, with himself at war,
  Forgets the shows of love to other men.
Cassius: Then, Brutus, I have much mistook your passion;
  By means whereof this breast of mine hath buried
  Thoughts of great value, worthy cogitations.   50
  Tell me, good Brutus, can you see your face?
Brutus: No, Cassius; for the eye sees not itself,
  But by reflection by some other things.
Cassius: 'Tis just:
  And it is very much lamented, Brutus,   55
  That you have no such mirrors as will turn
  Your hidden worthiness into your eye,
  That you might see your shadow. I have heard
  Where many of the best respect in Rome,

61   *yoke:* burden

71   *jealous on:* suspicious of

72-74   *Were I . . . protester:* If I were the kind of person who gave my friendship and loyalty to anyone who came along

76   *scandal:* slander

78   *rout:* boisterous, common mob

80   *king:* In 510 B.C. the Roman people, led by an ancestor of Brutus, rebelled against their tyrannical king, Tarquin the Proud. They vowed never again to accept a king as their ruler and, in 509 B.C., established a republic – a government in which power is held by the people or their elected representatives.

85   *aught:* anything

91   *outward favour:* appearance

95   *as lief not be:* just as soon not live

Except immortal Cæsar, speaking of Brutus   60
And groaning underneath this age's yoke,
Have wish'd that noble Brutus had his eyes.
Brutus: Into what dangers would you lead me, Cassius,
  That you would have me seek into myself
  For that which is not in me?   65
Cassius: Therefore, good Brutus, be prepared to hear:
  And since you know you cannot see yourself
  So well as by reflection, I, your glass,
  Will modestly discover to yourself
  That of yourself which you yet know not of.   70
  And be not jealous on me, gentle Brutus:
  Were I a common laugher, or did use
  To stale with ordinary oaths my love
  To every new protester; if you know
  That I do fawn on men and hug them hard   75
  And after scandal them; or if you know
  That I profess myself in banqueting
  To all the rout, then hold me dangerous.

                        [Flourish and shout.]

Brutus: What means this shouting? I do fear, the people
  Choose Cæsar for their king!
Cassius: Ay, do you fear it?   80
  Then must I think you would not have it so.
Brutus: I would not, Cassius; yet I love him well.
  But wherefore do you hold me here so long?
  What is it that you would impart to me?
  If it be aught toward the general good,   85
  Set honour in one eye and death i' th' other,
  And I will look on both indifferently:
  For let the gods so speed me as I love
  The name of honour more than I fear death.
Cassius: I know that virtue to be in you, Brutus,   90
  As well as I do know your outward favour.
  Well, honour is the subject of my story.
  I cannot tell what you and other men
  Think of this life; but, for my single self,
  I had as lief not be as live to be   95
  In awe of such a thing as I myself.
  I was born free as Cæsar; so were you:

105   *Accoutred:* dressed

109   *hearts of controversy:* spirit of competition

114   *Anchises bear:* Aeneas, a Trojan, was the founder of Rome.
        When Troy was captured and burned by the Greeks, Aeneas
        escaped from the city, carrying his father Anchises on his
        back.

122   *coward . . . fly:* the colour faded from his lips. The wording is
        suggestive of cowardly soldiers who desert their "colours" or flag.

123   *bend:* look

130   *start:* control

131   *palm:* victory. A crown of palm leaves was traditionally given to
        a conqueror or victor.

136   *Colossus:* an immense statue of the god Apollo

We both have fed as well, and we can both
Endure the winter's cold as well as he:
For once, upon a raw and gusty day, 100
The troubled Tiber chafing with her shores,
Cæsar said to me, "Darest thou, Cassius, now
Leap in with me into this angry flood,
And swim to yonder point?" Upon the word,
Accoutred as I was, I plunged in 105
And bade him follow; so indeed he did.
The torrent roared, and we did buffet it
With lusty sinews, throwing it aside
And stemming it with hearts of controversy;
But ere we could arrive the point proposed, 110
Cæsar cried, "Help me, Cassius, or I sink."
I, as Æneas our great ancestor
Did from the flames of Troy upon his shoulder
The old Anchises bear, so from the waves of Tiber
Did I the tired Cæsar: and this man 115
Is now become a god, and Cassius is
A wretched creature and must bend his body
If Cæsar carelessly but nod on him.
He had a fever when he was in Spain,
And when the fit was on him, I did mark 120
How he did shake: 'tis true, this god did shake:
His coward lips did from their colour fly,
And that same eye whose bend doth awe the world
Did lose his lustre: I did hear him groan:
Ay, and that tongue of his that bade the Romans 125
Mark him and write his speeches in their books,
Alas, it cried, "Give me some drink, Titinius,"
As a sick girl. Ye gods! it doth amaze me
A man of such a feeble temper should
So get the start of the majestic world 130
And bear the palm alone.   [*Shout. Flourish.*]
Brutus: Another general shout?
    I do believe that these applauses are
    For some new honours that are heap'd on Cæsar.
Cassius: Why, man, he doth bestride the narrow world 135
    Like a Colossus, and we petty men
    Walk under his huge legs and peep about

152   *the great flood:* Cassius is referring to an old classical story in which the god Zeus destroyed the world because people had become sinful. Only two people, a husband and wife, were saved because of their virtue.

159   *a Brutus:* Lucius Junius Brutus, the ancestor of Brutus who led the Romans to expel the Tarquins from Rome. *brook'd:* tolerated

163   *aim:* idea

170   *meet:* appropriate

171   *chew:* think, reflect

To find ourselves dishonourable graves.
Men at some time are masters of their fates:
The fault, dear Brutus, is not in our stars,   140
But in ourselves, that we are underlings.
Brutus and Cæsar: what should be in that Cæsar?
Why should that name be sounded more than yours?
Write them together, yours is as fair a name;
Sound them, it doth become the mouth as well;   145
Weigh them, it is as heavy; conjure with 'em,
Brutus will start a spirit as soon as Cæsar.
Now, in the names of all the gods at once,
Upon what meat doth this our Cæsar feed,
That he is grown so great? Age, thou art shamed!   150
Rome, thou hast lost the breed of noble bloods!
When went there by an age, since the great flood,
But it was famed with more than with one man?
When could they say till now, that talk'd of Rome,
That her wide walls encompass'd but one man?   155
Now is it Rome indeed, and room enough,
When there is in it but one only man.
O, you and I have heard our fathers say,
There was a Brutus once that would have brook'd
The eternal devil to keep his state in Rome   160
As easily as a king.
Brutus: That you do love me, I am nothing jealous;
What you would work me to, I have some aim:
How I have thought of this and of these times,
I shall recount hereafter; for this present,   165
I would not, so with love I might entreat you,
Be any further moved. What you have said
I will consider; what you have to say
I will with patience hear, and find a time
Both meet to hear and answer such high things.   170
Till then, my noble friend, chew upon this:
Brutus had rather be a villager
Than to repute himself a son of Rome
Under these hard conditions as this time
Is like to lay upon us.   175
Cassius: I am glad that my weak words
Have struck but thus much show of fire from Brutus.

186   *ferret:* a small animal with red eyes

188   *cross'd in conference:* challenged in debate

197   *well given:* a supporter (of Caesar's)

202-203 *he looks . . . men:* he sees through people's actions to their
         motives

Brutus: The games are done and Cæsar is returning.
Cassius: As they pass by, pluck Casca by the sleeve;
    And he will, after his sour fashion, tell you   180
    What hath proceeded worthy note to-day.

    [*Re-enter Cæsar and his train.*]

Brutus: I will do so. But, look you, Cassius,
    The angry spot doth glow on Cæsar's brow,
    And all the rest look like a chidden train:
    Calpurnia's cheek is pale; and Cicero   185
    Looks with such ferret and such fiery eyes
    As we have seen him in the Capitol,
    Being cross'd in conference by some senators.
Cassius: Casca will tell us what the matter is.
Cæsar: Antonius!   190
Antony: Cæsar?
Cæsar: Let me have men about me that are fat,
    Sleek-headed men, and such as sleep o'-nights:
    Yond Cassius has a lean and hungry look;
    He thinks too much: such men are dangerous.   195
Antony: Fear him not, Cæsar; he's not dangerous;
    He is a noble Roman and well given.
Cæsar: Would he were fatter. But I fear him not:
    Yet if my name were liable to fear,
    I do not know the man I should avoid   200
    So soon as that spare Cassius. He reads much;
    He is a great observer, and he looks
    Quite through the deeds of men; he loves no plays,
    As thou dost, Antony; he hears no music;
    Seldom he smiles, and smiles in such a sort   205
    As if he mock'd himself and scorn'd his spirit
    That could be moved to smile at anything.
    Such men as he be never at heart's ease
    While they behold a greater than themselves,
    And therefore are they very dangerous.   210
    I rather tell thee what is to be fear'd
    Than what I fear; for always I am Cæsar.
    Come on my right hand, for this ear is deaf,
    And tell me truly what thou think'st of him.
       [*Sennet. Exeunt Cæsar and his train. Casca remains.*]

216   *chanced:* happened

228   *marry:* truly (a mild oath, from "By the Virgin Mary")

235   *mark:* pay attention to

237   *coronets:* small crowns

243   *rabblement:* rabble, mob
244   *chopt:* chapped, rough

247   *swounded:* fainted

250   *But, soft:* Wait a minute.

Casca: You pulled me by the cloak; would you speak with
    me? 215
Brutus: Ay, Casca; tell us what hath chanced to-day,
That Cæsar looks so sad.
Casca: Why, you were with him, were you not?
Brutus: I should not then ask Casca what had chanced.
Casca: Why, there was a crown offered him: and being 220
    offered him, he put it by with the back of his hand,
    thus; and then the people fell a-shouting.
Brutus: What was the second noise for?
Casca: Why, for that too.
Cassius: They shouted thrice; what was the last cry for? 225
Casca: Why, for that too.
Brutus: Was the crown offered him thrice?
Casca: Ay, marry, was't, and he put it by thrice, every time
    gentler than other; and at every putting by mine
    honest neighbours shouted. 230
Cassius: Who offered him the crown?
Casca: Why, Antony.
Brutus: Tell us the manner of it, gentle Casca.
Casca: I can as well be hanged as tell the manner of it: it
    was mere foolery; I did not mark it. I saw Mark Antony 235
    offer him a crown; yet 'twas not a crown neither, 'twas
    one of these coronets; and, as I told you, he put it by
    once: but, for all that, to my thinking, he would fain
    have had it. Then he offered it to him again; then
    he put it by again: but, to my thinking, he was very 240
    loath to lay his fingers off it. And then he offered it
    the third time; he put it the third time by: and still as
    he refused it, the rabblement hooted and clapped their
    chopt hands and threw up their sweaty nightcaps, and
    uttered such a deal of stinking breath because Cæsar 245
    refused the crown, that it had almost choked Cæsar; for
    he swounded and fell down at it: and for mine own
    part, I durst not laugh, for fear of opening my lips and
    receiving the bad air.
Cassius: But, soft, I pray you: what, did Cæsar swound? 250
Casca: He fell down in the market-place, and foamed at
    mouth, and was speechless.
Brutus: 'Tis very like: he hath the falling sickness.

255   *falling sickness:* epilepsy

269   *amiss:* improper

272   *heed:* notice

Cassius: No, Cæsar hath it not; but you and I
And honest Casca, we have the falling sickness.   255
Casca: I know not what you mean by that; but, I am sure,
Cæsar fell down. If the tag-rag people did not clap him
and hiss him, according as he pleased and displeased
them, as they use to do the players in the theatre,
I am no true man.   260
Brutus: What said he when he came unto himself?
Casca: Marry, before he fell down, when he perceived the
common herd was glad he refused the crown, he
plucked me ope his doublet and offered them his throat
to cut. An I had been a man of any occupation, if I   265
would not have taken him at a word, I would I might
go to hell among the rogues. And so he fell. When
he came to himself again, he said, if he had done or said
any thing amiss, he desired their worships to think it
was his infirmity. Three or four wenches, where I stood,   270
cried, "Alas, good soul!" and forgave him with all their
hearts: but there's no heed to be taken of them; if Cæsar
had stabbed their mothers, they would have done
no less.
Brutus: And after that, he came, thus sad, away?   275
Casca: Ay.
Cassius: Did Cicero say anything?
Casca: Ay, he spoke Greek.
Cassius: To what effect?
Casca: Nay, and I tell you that, I'll ne'er look you i' th'   280
face again: but those that understood him smiled at one
another and shook their heads; but, for mine own
part, it was Greek to me. I could tell you more news
too: Marullus and Flavius, for pulling scarfs off
Cæsar's images, are put to silence. Fare you well.   285
There was more foolery yet, if I could remember it.
Cassius: Will you sup with me to-night, Casca?
Casca: No, I am promised forth.
Cassius: Will you dine with me to-morrow?
Casca: Ay, if I be alive and your mind hold and your dinner   290
worth the eating.
Cassius: Good: I will expect you.
Casca: Do so. Farewell both.   [*Exit.*]

295   *quick mettle:* full of spirit and enthusiasm

298   *tardy form:* appearance of being slow-witted

299   *This rudeness . . . wit:* His pretence of being stupid emphasizes his intelligence.

308   *wrought:* crafted, shaped

312   *bear me hard:* dislikes me

315   *several hands:* different handwritings

320   *seat him sure:* make his position secure, be careful

Brutus: What a blunt fellow is this grown to be!
  He was quick mettle when he went to school.   295
Cassius: So is he now in execution
  Of any bold or noble enterprise,
  However he puts on this tardy form.
  This rudeness is a sauce to his good wit,
  Which gives men stomach to digest his words   .   300
  With better appetite.
Brutus: And so it is. For this time I will leave you:
  To-morrow, if you please to speak with me,
  I will come home to you; or, if you will,
  Come home to me, and I will wait for you.   305
Cassius: I will do so: till then, think of the world.

                                    [Exit Brutus.]

  Well, Brutus, thou art noble; yet, I see,
  Thy honourable metal may be wrought
  From that it is disposed: therefore it is meet
  That noble minds keep ever with their likes;   310
  For who so firm that cannot be seduced?
  Cæsar doth bear me hard; but he loves Brutus:
  If I were Brutus now and he were Cassius,
  He should not humour me. I will this night,
  In several hands, in at his windows throw,   315
  As if they came from several citizens,
  Writings all tending to the great opinion
  That Rome holds of his name; wherein obscurely
  Cæsar's ambition should be glanced at:
  And after this let Cæsar seat him sure;   320
  For we will shake him, or worse days endure.

                                       [Exit.]

Act 1, Scene 2: Activities

1. In this scene, you have met Julius Caesar, both the private man and the public leader. What is your impression of Caesar? Discuss your ideas. Do you think the private man and the public man are different? Explain.

2. Imagine you are an "on-the-spot" reporter for a national television network. You are commenting upon the procession and opening events of this scene. Decide what important details of the setting and characters you want to highlight. Discuss your ideas with your group.

3. Casca reports events at the Capitol that Brutus, Cassius, and we, the audience, heard but did not see. From Casca's point of view, write a newspaper account of what happened.

4. Cassius tells us at the end of this scene that he is going to write letters to Brutus. What do you think he will say in the letters? What would you say to Brutus? Write a letter that you would send.

5. Write a horoscope prediction for Julius Caesar on his procession day, February 15, 44 BC. You will find examples in newspapers and magazines to use as models. Predict what will happen to him between this date and the Ides of March (March 15, 44 B.C.).

6. Caesar remarked to Antony that he does not trust Cassius's "lean and hungry look." How much does our appearance reveal about us? Find several pictures of people whose faces suggest their personalities and the sorts of experiences they may have had. Display your collection and share your ideas with your viewers.

7. Discuss your impressions of Cassius with a partner using evidence from the scene to support your opinion. Create a profile of Cassius in your journal. As you continue to

explore the play, add to your profile of Cassius. Decide whether the new information you gain changes your opinion of him.

8. In groups, discuss your answers to the following questions:
   - Is Brutus an effective officer of the Roman government? Why or why not?
   - Whom would you rather have as a friend, Cassius or Brutus?
   - Is there a difference between the Cassius we see in conversation with others and the Cassius who speaks the soliloquy at the end of the scene? Explain.

9. Brutus apologizes to Cassius for hiding his true self, explaining that he has been preoccupied (lines 37–42). Think of a situation you know in which a friend with a problem acted unlike his or her usual self. Write a letter to the person in which you describe the troubled person you saw and the real person you know.

For the next scene . . .

Do you believe in omens (signs of events that will happen)? There have been many accounts of people reporting the occurrence of strange phenomena (facts or events as they appear to the senses) just before some significant event, good or bad, took place. Have you ever had or do you know someone who has had such an experience? If so, share it with your group.

Act 1, Scene 3

In this scene . . .

On the eve of the Ides of March, a violent storm rages throughout Rome. A frightened Casca meets with Cicero and reports a strange phenomenon that he has witnessed. Later, Cassius arrives and uses these events to advance his plans for putting the conspiracy into action.

The plan to crown Caesar proves to be an important factor for Cassius's cause. He, along with Casca and Cinna, formulate plans for events that will soon lead to other kinds of storms.

6 *rived:* split

26 *bird of night:* owl

28 *prodigies:* unnatural events

Scene 3

Rome. A street.

Thunder and lightning. Enter, from opposite sides, Casca, with his sword drawn, and Cicero.

Cicero: Good even, Casca: brought you Cæsar home?
  Why are you breathless? And why stare you so?
Casca: Are not you moved, when all the sway of earth
  Shakes like a thing unfirm? O Cicero,
  I have seen tempests, when the scolding winds   5
  Have rived the knotty oaks, and I have seen
  The ambitious ocean swell and rage and foam,
  To be exalted with the threatening clouds:
  But never till to-night, never till now,
  Did I go through a tempest dropping fire.   10
  Either there is a civil strife in heaven,
  Or else the world, too saucy with the gods,
  Incenses them to send destruction.
Cicero: Why, saw you anything more wonderful?
Casca: A common slave, you know him well by sight,   15
  Held up his left hand, which did flame and burn
  Like twenty torches join'd, and yet his hand,
  Not sensible of fire, remained unscorch'd.
  Besides—I ha' not since put up my sword—
  Against the Capitol I met a lion,   20
  Who glared upon me, and went surly by
  Without annoying me: and there were drawn
  Upon a heap a hundred ghastly women
  Transformed with their fear, who swore they saw
  Men all in fire walk up and down the streets.   25
  And yesterday the bird of night did sit
  Even at noon-day upon the market-place,
  Hooting and shrieking. When these prodigies

29   *conjointly meet:* coincide

31   *portentous:* foreboding, threatening

48   *unbraced:* with shirt unfastened

56   *heralds:* omens

58   *want:* lack

Do so conjointly meet, let not men say
"These are their reasons: they are natural"; 30
For, I believe, they are portentous things
Unto the climate that they point upon.
Cicero: Indeed, it is a strange-disposed time:
But men may construe things after their fashion,
Clean from the purpose of the things themselves. 35
Comes Cæsar to the Capitol to-morrow?
Casca: He doth; for he did bid Antonius
Send word to you he would be there to-morrow.
Cicero: Good-night, then, Casca; this disturbed sky
Is not to walk in.
Casca: Farewell, Cicero.   [*Exit Cicero.*] 40

[*Enter Cassius.*]

Cassius: Who's there?
Casca: A Roman.
Cassius: Casca, by your voice.
Casca: Your ear is good, Cassius, what night is this!
Cassius: A very pleasing night to honest men.
Casca: Who ever knew the heavens menace so?
Cassius: Those that have known the earth so full of faults. 45
For my part, I have walk'd about the streets,
Submitting me unto the perilous night,
And thus unbraced, Casca, as you see,
Have bared my bosom to the thunder-stone;
And when the cross blue lightning seem'd to open 50
The breast of heaven, I did present myself
Even in the aim and very flash of it.
Casca: But wherefore did you so much tempt the heavens?
It is the part of men to fear and tremble,
When the most mighty gods by tokens send 55
Such dreadful heralds to astonish us.
Cassius: You are dull, Casca, and those sparks of life
That should be in a Roman you do want,
Or else you use not. You look pale and gaze
And put on fear and cast yourself in wonder, 60
To see the strange impatience of the heavens:
But if you would consider the true cause
Why all these fires, why all these gliding ghosts,

64   *from quality and kind:* against their natures

66   *ordinance:* natural ways of behaving

77   *prodigious:* threatening

81   *thews:* sinews, muscles

84   *yoke and sufferance:* endurance of this burden

95   *be retentive to:* hold in

101   *bondman:* slave

Why birds and beasts from quality and kind,
Why old men fool and children calculate, 65
Why all these things change from their ordinance
Their natures and preformed faculties,
To monstrous quality, why, you shall find
That heaven hath infused them with these spirits,
To make them instruments of fear and warning 70
Unto some monstrous state.
Now could I, Casca, name to thee a man
Most like this dreadful night,
That thunders, lightens, opens graves, and roars
As doth the lion in the Capitol, 75
A man no mightier than thyself or me
In personal action, yet prodigious grown
And fearful, as these strange eruptions are.
Casca: 'Tis Cæsar that you mean; is it not, Cassius?
Cassius: Let it be who it is: for Romans now 80
Have thews and limbs like to their ancestors;
But, woe the while! our fathers' minds are dead,
And we are govern'd with our mothers' spirits;
Our yoke and sufferance show us womanish.
Casca: Indeed, they say the senators to-morrow 85
Mean to establish Cæsar as a king;
And he shall wear his crown by sea and land,
In every place, save here in Italy.
Cassius: I know where I will wear this dagger then:
Cassius from bondage will deliver Cassius: 90
Therein, ye gods, you make the weak most strong;
Therein, ye gods, you tyrants do defeat:
Nor stony tower, nor walls of beaten brass,
Nor airless dungeon, nor strong links of iron,
Can be retentive to the strength of spirit; 95
But life, being weary of these worldly bars,
Never lacks power to dismiss itself.
If I know this, know all the world besides,
That part of tyranny that I do bear
I can shake off at pleasure.   [*Thunder still.*]
Casca: So can I: 100
So every bondman in his own hand bears
The power to cancel his captivity.

106   *hinds:* female deer

109   *offal:* waste, garbage

117   *fleering:* sneering, scornful
118   *Be factious for redress:* form a group to challenge or correct

125   *by this they stay:* by now they are waiting
126   *Pompey's porch:* an open park-like area in front of the theatre built by Pompey

135-136 *incorporate to our attempts:* joining us in the conspiracy

Cassius: And why should Cæsar be a tyrant then?
Poor man! I know he would not be a wolf,
But that he sees the Romans are but sheep: 105
He were no lion, were not Romans hinds.
Those that with haste will make a mighty fire
Begin it with weak straws: what trash is Rome,
What rubbish and what offal, when it serves
For the base matter to illuminate   110
So vile a thing as Cæsar! But, O grief,
Where hast thou led me? I perhaps speak this
Before a willing bondman; then I know
My answer must be made. But I am arm'd,
And dangers are to me indifferent.   115
Casca: You speak to Casca, and to such a man
That is no fleering tell-tale. Hold, my hand:
Be factious for redress of all these griefs,
And I will set this foot of mine as far
As who goes farthest.
Cassius: There's a bargain made.   120
Now know you, Casca, I have moved already
Some certain of the noblest-minded Romans
To undergo with me an enterprise
Of honourable-dangerous consequence;
And I do know, by this they stay for me   125
In Pompey's porch: for now, this fearful night,
There is no stir or walking in the streets;
And the complexion of the element
Is feverous like the work we have in hand,
Most bloody-fiery, and most terrible.   130

[*Enter Cinna.*]

Casca: Stand close awhile, for here comes one in haste.
Cassius: 'Tis Cinna; I do know him by his gait;
He is a friend. Cinna, where haste you so?
Cinna: To find out you. Who's that? Metellus Cimber?
Cassius: No, it is Casca; one incorporate   135
To our attempts. Am I not stay'd for, Cinna?
Cinna: I am glad on't. What a fearful night is this!
There's two or three of us have seen strange sights.
Cassius: Am I not stay'd for? tell me.

143   *praetor's chair:* the official chair in which Brutus sat as chief magistrate

145   *set this up with wax:* seal

150   *hie:* hurry

153   *ere:* before

159   *countenance:* support; *alchemy:* early science of chemistry, especially the attempts to change common metals such as lead and tin into gold

162   *conceited:* understood

Cinna: Yes, you are.   140
  O Cassius, if you could
  But win the noble Brutus to our party——
Cassius: Be you content: good Cinna, take this paper,
  And look you lay it in the prætor's chair,
  Where Brutus may but find it; and throw this
  In at his window; set this up with wax   145
  Upon old Brutus' statue: all this done,
  Repair to Pompey's porch, where you shall find us.
  Is Decius Brutus and Trebonius there?
Cinna: All but Metellus Cimber; and he's gone
  To seek you at your house. Well, I will hie,   150
  And so bestow these papers as you bade me.
Cassius: That done, repair to Pompey's theatre.
                              [*Exit Cinna.*]
  Come, Casca, you and I will yet ere day
  See Brutus at his house: three parts of him
  Is ours already, and the man entire   155
  Upon the next encounter yields him ours.
Casca: O, he sits high in all the people's hearts:
  And that which would appear offence in us,
  His countenance, like richest alchemy,
  Will change to virtue and to worthiness.   160
Cassius: Him and his worth and our great need of him
  You have right well conceited. Let us go,
  For it is after midnight, and ere day
  We will awake him and be sure of him.   [*Exeunt.*]

Act 1, Scene 3: Activities

1. Recall a story, film, or dramatic production you know in which the weather conditions accompanying an important event have a significant role in the development of the action. Describe the relationship between the weather and the events. Compare the effect the storm in this scene has with the situation you described. How are they the same? different?

2. Consider Cassius's behaviour in this scene. What additional information about his character is revealed? What is the evidence for this? Note your findings in your journal and look for further evidence in later scenes that will either verify or change your opinion.

3. If you had to choose either Cassius or Casca to help you get elected to the executive of the Student Council or some other organization of which you are a member, which one of them would you choose? Why? Write a letter to him asking for his assistance. Outline the ways in which you would like him to support you in becoming elected.

4. Think of an important social or political event such as a wedding or an election, that is about to take place where you live. Prepare a dialogue between two characters in which they discuss their predictions about the event. Decide what mood or atmosphere you wish to create for the conversation and select appropriate music. Rehearse your dialogue with a classmate, tape it, and present your tape to an audience.

Act 1: Consider the Whole Act

1. In groups of four or five, offer your opinions about one of the characters in this act. Formulate three or four sentences about the character, including details you have gained about the character's physical features and behaviour.

   With your group, create a portrait gallery of these major characters by posting selected descriptions on the bulletin board.

   Find a newspaper or magazine picture of a person whose appearance and expression suggest a modern-day image of your chosen character. Place this picture above the description posted on the bulletin board.

2. Prepare a list of about five questions which you would like to ask a character in this act. Phrase the questions so that they will require the character to reveal as much of his personality as possible.
   - In your group, conduct an interview having one person ask the questions and a second person play the character. Limit your interviews to three to five minutes.
   - Have your group evaluate the success of your questions on the basis of the quality of the answers they draw from the character.
   - Tape your interviews to refer to in later activities.

3. Select a part of a scene in this act that includes two or more characters and ten or more lines of text. As a director, choose whom you will cast for each role.
   - Decide what main points you wish to communicate to your audience.
   - As you rehearse the scene, make certain that you are clear about the meaning of the lines, the interpretation you wish to give them, the movements of the characters and the interaction taking place among them.
   - Decide what, if any, props and costume items you need.

After you have presented your scene, discuss with your audience what they consider to be the major strengths of your presentation. Ask them to suggest ways in which you could improve your work.

4. Read through the notes and journal entries you have made for this act and write a summary of your response to the act. Use the following questions to help you:
   - What have I discovered about the life and conditions of Rome in 44 B.C. for the common people? for the political figures?
   - What have I learned about (a character that interests me)?
   - What are some interesting effects created for the audience in one of the scenes?

5. If you were an advisor to Caesar, what would you say to him about:
   - the warning from the Soothsayer about the Ides of March.
   - his own observations on Cassius.
   - his three-time refusal of the crown.

   Choose a partner and, acting as the advisor, create a conversation that will include these comments. Present your conversation to an audience.

For the next scene . . .

Think of a time when you were faced with a serious problem
that required you to make an important decision. What did
you do? How did you feel?

Act 2, Scene 1

In this scene . . .

It is early in the morning of the Ides of March, and Brutus is in his orchard. As the thunder still sounds in the distance and the last flashes of lightning illumine the dark sky, we learn about the storm that is raging within Brutus. He has made his decision and attempts to justify it by giving his reasons. Soon the conspirators arrive and final plans for the assassination of Caesar are discussed and arranged. When Brutus is once again alone, his wife Portia enters. She urges him to share with her what is troubling him. Their conversation is interrupted by the arrival of the ailing Ligarius, who pledges his loyalty to Brutus. The two men then leave together for Caesar's house.

11   *spurn at:* reject, repel

12   *general:* the public welfare

19   *Remorse:* mercy, compassion

20   *affections:* emotions

28-29   *the quarrel . . . he is:* there is no reason or cause to complain
        about what he is now

Act 2, Scene 1

Rome. Brutus' orchard.

Enter Brutus.

Brutus: What, Lucius, ho!
  I cannot, by the progress of the stars,
  Give guess how near to day. Lucius, I say!
  I would it were my fault to sleep so soundly.
  When, Lucius, when? awake, I say! what, Lucius!   5

[*Enter Lucius.*]

Lucius: Call'd you, my lord?
Brutus: Get me a taper in my study, Lucius:
  When it is lighted, come and call me here.
Lucius: I will, my lord.   [*Exit.*]
Brutus: It must be by his death: and, for my part,   10
  I know no personal cause to spurn at him,
  But for the general. He would be crown'd:
  How that might change his nature, there's the question.
  It is the bright day that brings forth the adder;
  And that craves wary walking. Crown him?—that;—   15
  And then, I grant, we put a sting in him,
  That at his will he may do danger with.
  The abuse of greatness is when it disjoins
  Remorse from power: and, to speak truth of Cæsar,
  I have not known when his affections sway'd   20
  More than his reason. But 'tis a common proof,
  That lowliness is young ambition's ladder,
  Whereto the climber-upward turns his face;
  But when he once attains the upmost round,
  He then unto the ladder turns his back,   25
  Looks in the clouds, scorning the base degrees
  By which he did ascend: so Cæsar may;
  Then, lest he may, prevent. And, since the quarrel

30   *augmented:* increased, enlarged

44   *exhalations:* meteors

47   *redress:* remedy, set right

52   *under one man's awe:* in respect and fear of one man

Will bear no colour for the thing he is,
Fashion it thus; that what he is, augmented,   30
Would run to these and these extremities:
And therefore think him as a serpent's egg
Which, hatch'd, would, as his kind, grow mischievous,
And kill him in the shell.

[*Re-enter Lucius.*]

Lucius: The taper burneth in your closet, sir.   35
 Searching the window for a flint I found
 This paper thus seal'd up, and I am sure
 It did not lie there when I went to bed.
                                        [*Gives him the letter.*]
Brutus: Get you to bed again; it is not day.
 Is not to-morrow, boy, the Ides of March?   40
Lucius: I know not, sir.
Brutus: Look in the calendar, and bring me word.
Lucius: I will, sir.   [*Exit.*]
Brutus: The exhalations whizzing in the air
 Give so much light that I may read by them.   45
                                    [*Opens the letter and reads.*]
  "Brutus, thou sleep'st: awake and see thyself.
  Shall Rome, etc. Speak, strike, redress!
  Brutus, thou sleep'st: awake!"
Such instigations have been often dropp'd
Where I have took them up.   50
"Shall Rome, etc." Thus must I piece it out:
Shall Rome stand under one man's awe? What, Rome?
My ancestors did from the streets of Rome
The Tarquin drive, when he was call'd a king.
"Speak, strike, redress!" Am I entreated   55
To speak and strike? O Rome, I make thee promise,
If the redress will follow, thou receivest
Thy full petition at the hand of Brutus!

[*Re-enter Lucius.*]

Lucius: Sir, March is wasted fourteen days.
                                        [*Knocking within.*]
Brutus: 'Tis good. Go to the gate; somebody knocks.   60
                                        [*Exit Lucius.*]

65   *phantasma:* hallucination

66   *The Genius . . . instruments:* an immortal spirit or angel (genius) was thought to rule people through the use of mortal faculties (bodily powers which included the emotions, the will, and the ability to reason)

67   *in council:* at war. Brutus is suggesting that he is in conflict with the immortal spirit which decides what will happen.

76   *mark of favour:* distinguishing features

82   *affability:* friendliness

83   *for if . . . on:* if you walk showing your true appearance

84   *Erebus:* In Greek mythology this was the dark region underneath the earth through which the dead passed on their way to Hades, the underworld.

85   *from prevention:* from being stopped

Since Cassius first did whet me against Cæsar,
I have not slept.
Between the acting of a dreadful thing
And the first motion, all the interim is
Like a phantasma or a hideous dream: 65
The Genius and the mortal instruments
Are then in council; and the state of man,
Like to a little kingdom, suffers then
The nature of an insurrection.

[*Re-enter Lucius*]

Lucius: Sir, 'tis your brother Cassius at the door,   70
    Who doth desire to see you.
Brutus: Is he alone?
Lucius: No, sir, there are moe with him.
Brutus: Do you know them?
Lucius: No, sir; their hats are pluck'd about their ears,
    And half their faces buried in their cloaks,
    That by no means I may discover them   75
    By any mark of favour.
Brutus: Let 'em enter.   [*Exit Lucius.*]
    They are the faction. O conspiracy,
    Shamest thou to show thy dangerous brow by night,
    When evils are most free? O, then, by day
    Where wilt thou find a cavern dark enough   80
    To mask thy monstrous visage? Seek none, conspiracy;
    Hide it in smiles and affability:
    For if thou path, thy native semblance on,
    Not Erebus itself were dim enough
    To hide thee from prevention.   85

[*Enter the Conspirators, Cassius, Casca, Decius, Cinna,
    Metellus Cimber, and Trebonius.*]

Cassius: I think we are too bold upon your rest:
    Good-morrow, Brutus; do we trouble you?
Brutus: I have been up this hour, awake all night.
    Know I these men that come along with you?
Cassius: Yes, every man of them: and no man here   90
    But honours you; and every one doth wish
    You had but that opinion of yourself

104   *fret:* streak across

115   *sufferance:* endurance

118   *high-sighted:* arrogant

126   *palter:* hesitate

129   *cautelous:* deceitful

130   *carrions:* creatures almost dead and rotting

Which every noble Roman bears of you.
This is Trebonius.
Brutus: He is welcome hither.
Cassius: This, Decius Brutus.
Brutus: He is welcome too.   95
Cassius: This, Casca; this, Cinna; and this, Metellus Cimber.
Brutus: They are all welcome.
What watchful cares do interpose themselves
Betwixt your eyes and night?
Cassius: Shall I entreat a word?   [*They whisper.*] 100
Decius: Here lies the east: doth not the day break here?
Casca: No.
Cinna: O, pardon, sir, it doth; and yon grey lines
That fret the clouds are messengers of day.
Casca: You shall confess that you are both deceived.   105
Here, as I point my sword, the sun arises;
Which is a great way growing on the south,
Weighing the youthful season of the year.
Some two months hence up higher toward the north
He first presents his fire; and the high east   110
Stands, as the Capitol, directly here.
Brutus: Give me your hands all over, one by one.
Cassius: And let us swear our resolution.
Brutus: No, not an oath: if not the face of men,
The sufferance of our souls, the time's abuse,—   115
If these be motives weak, break off betimes,
And every man hence to his idle bed;
So let high-sighted tyranny range on,
Till each man drop by lottery. But if these,
As I am sure they do, bear fire enough   120
To kindle cowards and to steel with valour
The melting spirits of women, then, countrymen,
What need we any spur but our own cause
To prick us to redress? what other bond
Than secret Romans, that have spoke the word,   125
And will not palter? and what other oath
Than honesty to honesty engaged
That this shall be, or we will fall for it?
Swear priests and cowards and men cautelous,
Old feeble carrions and such suffering souls   130

138   *of a several bastardy:* not being pure Roman blood, i.e., not
       being of true Roman spirit and character

150   *break with:* confide in

155   *urged:* suggested

160   *annoy:* harm

164   *envy:* malice

That welcome wrongs; unto bad causes swear
Such creatures as men doubt; but do not stain
The even virtue of our enterprise,
Nor the insuppressive mettle of our spirits,
To think that or our cause or our performance   135
Did need an oath; when every drop of blood
That every Roman bears, and nobly bears,
Is guilty of a several bastardy,
If he do break the smallest particle
Of any promise that hath pass'd from him.   140
Cassius: But what of Cicero? shall we sound him?
  I think he will stand very strong with us.
Casca: Let us not leave him out.
Cinna: No, by no means.
Metellus: O, let us have him, for his silver hairs
  Will purchase us a good opinion,   145
  And buy men's voices to commend our deeds:
  It shall be said, his judgment ruled our hands;
  Our youths and wildness shall no whit appear,
  But all be buried in his gravity.
Brutus: O, name him not: let us not break with him: 150
  For he will never follow anything
  That other men begin.
Cassius: Then leave him out.
Casca: Indeed he is not fit.
Decius: Shall no man else be touch'd but only Cæsar?
Cassius: Decius, well urged: I think it is not meet, 155
  Mark Antony, so well beloved of Cæsar,
  Should outlive Cæsar: we shall find of him
  A shrewd contriver; and you know, his means,
  If he improve them, may well stretch so far
  As to annoy us all: which to prevent,   160
  Let Antony and Cæsar fall together.
Brutus: Our course will seem too bloody, Caius Cassius,
  To cut the head off and then hack the limbs,
  Like wrath in death and envy afterwards;
  For Antony is but a limb of Cæsar: 165
  Let us be sacrificers, but not butchers, Caius.
  We all stand up against the spirit of Cæsar;
  And in the spirit of men there is no blood:

175   *subtle:* crafty

179   *common eyes:* the general public

180   *purgers:* healers, cleansers

184   *ingrafted:* strongly rooted

188   *that were much:* that would be difficult for him to do

196   *Quite from the main opinion:* very different from the strong opinion

197   *ceremonies:* religious practices that predict the future

198   *prodigies:* signs of disaster

200   *augurers:* a group of religious officials who foretold the future from omens

O, that we then could come by Cæsar's spirit,
And not dismember Cæsar! But, alas!   170
Cæsar must bleed for it! And, gentle friends.
Let's kill him boldly, but not wrathfully;
Let's carve him as a dish fit for the gods,
Not hew him as a carcase fit for hounds:
And let our hearts, as subtle masters do,   175
Stir up their servants to an act of rage,
And after seem to chide 'em. This shall make
Our purpose necessary and not envious:
Which so appearing to the common eyes,
We shall be call'd purgers, not murderers.   180
And for Mark Antony, think not of him;
For he can do no more than Cæsar's arm
When Cæsar's head is off.
Cassius: Yet I fear him;
For in the ingrafted love he bears to Cæsar——
Brutus: Alas! good Cassius, do not think of him.   185
If he love Cæsar, all that he can do
Is to himself, take thought and die for Cæsar:
And that were much he should, for he is given
To sports, to wildness, and much company.
Trebonius: There is no fear in him; let him not die; 190
For he will live, and laugh at this hereafter.
                                   [*Clock strikes.*]
Brutus: Peace! count the clock.
Cassius: The clock hath stricken three.
Trebonius: 'Tis time to part.
Cassius: But it is doubtful yet
Whether Cæsar will come forth to-day, or no;
For he is superstitious grown of late,   195
Quite from the main opinion he held once
Of fantasy, of dreams and ceremonies:
It may be, these apparent prodigies,
The unaccustom'd terror of this night,
And the persuasion of his augurers,   200
May hold him from the Capitol to-day.
Decius: Never fear that: if he be so resolved,
I can o'ersway him; for he loves to hear
That unicorns may be betray'd with trees,

204-206 *That unicorns . . . toils:* It was believed that a hunter should stand
behind a tree to catch a unicorn. When the unicorn charged,
it would drive its horn into the tree and be captured. It was also
thought that a bear would be so occupied with gazing at its
reflection in a mirror that a hunter could catch it easily. Elephants
were caught in holes lightly covered with branches and lions
were caught by hidden snares.

210 *bent:* direction

215 *bear Caesar hard:* hold a grudge against Caesar

216 *rated:* scolded

220 *fashion him:* shape him to our purposes; persuade him to become a member of our conspiracy

225 *put on:* display, reveal

231 *no figures nor no fantasies:* no problems or imaginings

And bears with glasses, elephants with holes,   205
Lions with toils and men with flatterers;
But when I tell him he hates flatterers,
He says he does, being then most flattered.
Let me work;
For I can give his humour the true bent,   210
And I will bring him to the Capitol.
Cassius: Nay, we will all of us be there to fetch him.
Brutus: By the eighth hour: is that the uttermost?
Cinna: Be that the uttermost, and fail not then.
Metellus: Caius Ligarius doth bear Cæsar hard,   215
Who rated him for speaking well of Pompey:
I wonder none of you have thought of him.
Brutus: Now, good Metellus, go along by him:
He loves me well, and I have given him reasons;
Send him but hither, and I'll fashion him.   220
Cassius: The morning comes upon's: we'll leave you, Brutus.
And, friends, disperse yourselves; but all remember
What you have said, and show yourselves true Romans.
Brutus: Good gentlemen, look fresh and merrily;
Let not our looks put on our purposes;   225
But bear it as our Roman actors do,
With untired spirits and formal constancy:
And so, good morrow to you every one.
                                    [*Exeunt. Brutus remains.*]
Boy! Lucius! Fast asleep? It is no matter;
Enjoy the honey-heavy dew of slumber: 230
Thou hast no figures nor no fantasies,
Which busy care draws in the brains of men;
Therefore thou sleep'st so sound.

[*Enter Portia.*]

Portia: Brutus, my lord!
Brutus: Portia, what mean you? wherefore rise you now?
It is not for your health thus to commit   235
Your weak condition to the raw cold morning.
Portia: Nor for yours neither. You've ungently, Brutus,
Stole from my bed: and yesternight, at supper,
You suddenly arose and walk'd about,
Musing and sighing, with your arms across;   240

246   *wafture:* wave

249   *withal:* also, at the same time
250   *an effect of humour:* a temporary mood

259   *embrace the means:* take the necessary steps

262   *humours:* dampness, mist

266   *rheumy:* cold and damp

275   *heavy:* disturbed

And when I ask'd you what the matter was,
You stared upon me with ungentle looks;
I urged you further, then you scratch'd your head,
And too impatiently stamp'd with your foot;
Yet I insisted, yet you answer'd not,   245
But, with an angry wafture of your hand,
Gave sign for me to leave you: so I did,
Fearing to strengthen that impatience
Which seem'd too much enkindled, and withal
Hoping it was but an effect of humour,   250
Which sometime hath his hour with every man.
It will not let you eat, nor talk, nor sleep
And could it work so much upon your shape
As it hath much prevail'd on your condition,
I should not know you, Brutus. Dear my lord,   255
Make me acquainted with your cause of grief.
Brutus: I am not well in health, and that is all.
Portia: Brutus is wise, and, were he not in health,
He would embrace the means to come by it.
Brutus: Why, so I do. Good Portia, go to bed.   260
Portia: Is Brutus sick? and is it physical
To walk unbraced and suck up the humours
Of the dark morning? What, is Brutus sick,
And will he steal out of his wholesome bed,
To dare the vile contagion of the night   265
And tempt the rheumy and unpurged air
To add unto his sickness? No, my Brutus;
You have some sick offence within your mind,
Which, by the right and virtue of my place,
I ought to know of: and, upon my knees,   270
I charm you, by my once commended beauty,
By all your vows of love and that great vow
Which did incorporate and make us one,
That you unfold to me, your self, your half,
Why you are heavy, and what men to-night   275
Have had resort to you: for here have been
Some six or seven, who did hide their faces
Even from darkness.
Brutus: Kneel not, gentle Portia.

289   *ruddy drops:* blood

295   *Cato:* Portia's father, Marcus Cato (95 B.C. – 46 B.C.) was highly respected for his courage and integrity. He was devoted to the Republic of Rome and had fought with Pompey against Caesar.

299   *constancy:* capacity to endure pain and suffering

308   *charactery:* the lines and wrinkles that are written (on my forehead)

313   *Vouchsafe:* may I say

Portia: I should not need, if you were gentle Brutus.
    Within the bond of marriage, tell me, Brutus,   280
    Is it excepted I should know no secrets
    That appertain to you? Am I yourself
    But, as it were, in sort or limitation,
    To keep with you at meals, comfort your bed,
    And talk to you sometimes? Dwell I but in the suburbs   285
    Of your good pleasure? If it be no more,
    Portia is Brutus's harlot, not his wife.
Brutus: You are my true and honourable wife,
    As dear to me as are the ruddy drops
    That visit my sad heart.   290
Portia: If this were true, then should I know this secret.
    I grant I am a woman; but withal
    A woman that Lord Brutus took to wife:
    I grant I am a woman; but withal
    A woman well-reputed, Cato's daughter.   295
    Think you I am no stronger than my sex,
    Being so father'd and so husbanded?
    Tell me your counsels, I will not disclose 'em:
    I have made strong proof of my constancy,
    Giving myself a voluntary wound   300
    Here in the thigh: can I bear that with patience,
    And not my husband's secrets?
Brutus: O ye gods,
    Render me worthy of this noble wife!

                        [Knocking within.]
    Hark, hark! one knocks: Portia, go in awhile;
    And by and by thy bosom shall partake   305
    The secrets of my heart.
    All my engagements I will construe to thee
    All the charactery of my sad brows:
    Leave me with haste. *[Exit Portia,]* Lucius, who's that
      knocks?

[Re-enter Lucius followed by Ligarius.]

Lucius: Here is a sick man that would speak with you.   310
Brutus: Caius Ligarius, that Metellus spake of.
    Boy, stand aside, Caius Ligarius! how?
Ligarius: Vouchsafe good morrow from a feeble tongue.

315   *To wear a kerchief:* to be ill. When people were sick they wore scarves or head covers for protection from drafts.

323   *exorcist:* a person who casts out evil spirits

Brutus: O, what a time have you chose out, brave Caius,
  To wear a kerchief! Would you were not sick! 315
Ligarius: I am not sick, if Brutus have in hand
  Any exploit worthy the name of honour.
Brutus: Such an exploit have I in hand, Ligarius,
  Had you a healthful ear to hear of it.
Ligarius: By all the gods that Romans bow before, 320
  I here discard my sickness! Soul of Rome?
  Brave son, derived from honourable loins!
  Thou, like an exorcist hast conjured up
  My mortified spirit. Now bid me run,
  And I will strive with things impossible; 325
  Yea, get the better of them. What's to do?
Brutus: A piece of work that will make sick men whole.
Ligarius: But are not some whole that we must make sick?
Brutus: That must we also. What it is, my Caius,
  I shall unfold to thee, as we are going 330
  To whom it must be done.
Ligarius: Set on your foot,
  And with a heart new-fired I follow you,
  To do I know not what: but it sufficeth
  That Brutus leads me on.   [*Thunder.*]
Brutus: Follow me then.   [*Exeunt.*]

Act 2, Scene 1: Activities

1. Soliloquies are speeches in which actors talk to the audience about themselves and reveal their intentions. Reread Brutus's soliloquy, "It must be death" (lines 10–34). In a group, discuss your ideas about the following:
   - what reasons Brutus had for joining the conspirators
   - your feelings about his decision and his reasoning
   - whether you think his soliloquy is believable
   - what there is about his soliloquy that may account for your feelings

   You may wish to share your opinions with other groups in your class. Write these new ideas about Brutus to a profile of him that you develop.

2. Do you think Brutus is the kind of person who would seek other people's opinions or advice? Give evidence to support your opinion.
   - If you were to offer Brutus advice, what would you say to him? Would it be spoken or written?
   - Tell Brutus what you think about his decision and the line of reasoning he follows in his soliloquy.

   Talk about your ideas with your group.

3. After Brutus welcomes the conspirators, he and Cassius have their own private conversation. No one hears what they say to each other. Imagine you are in a position to eavesdrop on the discussion. Create a dialogue between Cassius and Brutus. Share your dialogue with members of your group.

4. After seeing Brutus come to his decision to murder Caesar, examine his reasoning in making other decisions in this scene, such as his decision to leave Cicero out of the conspiracy. Discuss your discoveries with other members of your group or class.

   In your journal, add your ideas about Brutus to the profile you have been developing.

5. Do you think Brutus and the other conspirators would make sound leaders of government in a Rome without Caesar? Write a political commentary for a Roman newspaper explaining why you think they would make a superior/inferior government.

6. In terms of her time on stage and the number of lines she says, Portia's role is a small one, yet many actresses are eager to play this role.

   If you were a casting director, what actress that you know would you choose to play Portia? Why?

7. Consider ways in which lighting, colour and shadow are used in one or more of your favourite television programs or films. What lighting effects could be used for this scene to emphasize the action and intensify its atmosphere and moods? Discuss the suggestions you could give to the lighting director.

8. Stage a part of the scene (ten or more lines) that includes Brutus, Cassius, and the other conspirators. Plan the staging of the action to show the relationship that has developed between Brutus and the others. When rehearsing the segment, use a checklist that includes notes on the following:
   • Where will Brutus and Cassius stand in relation to each other? How will they use the space between them?
   • Where will the other characters stand in relation to Brutus and Cassius? How will they act and react to what is going on?

For the next scene . . .

Have you ever been flattered by another person or group of people? What were the circumstances and how did you react? Record your experience in your journal. Explain how you think flattery can be a positive influence on a person and how it might be a negative one.

Act 2, Scene 2

In this scene . . .

We discover a sleepless Caesar troubled by the raging storm and Calpurnia's dreams of his murder. After asking the augurers (priests who interpret omens) to predict his fortune for that day, he says that he plans to go to the Capitol despite his wife's pleadings for him to stay home. Even after he hears the report from the augurers warning him not "to stir forth today", Caesar states that he is still not afraid. Nevertheless, he soon bows to Calpurnia's wishes. Decius arrives, however, and convinces Caesar that he *must* go to the Capitol. When the rest of the conspirators enter, Caesar greets them graciously, and soon they leave for the Capitol.

6   *success:* the result of the sacrifice. Priests would sacrifice animals to the gods and interpret the appearance of the entrails (inner organs) to predict the future.

13   *stood on ceremonies:* believed in omens

25   *beyond all use:* unnatural, beyond everything we are accustomed to seeing

Scene 2

*The same. A room in
Cæsar's house.*

*Thunder and lightning. Enter Cæsar
in his nightgown.*

Cæsar: Nor heaven nor earth have been at peace tonight:
   Thrice hath Calpurnia in her sleep cried out,
   "Help, ho! they murder Cæsar!" Who's within?

[*Enter a Servant.*]

Servant: My lord?
Cæsar: Go bid the priests do present sacrifice   5
   And bring me their opinions of success.
Servant: I will, my lord.   [*Exit.*]

[*Enter Calpurnia.*]

Calpurnia: What mean you, Cæsar? think you to walk forth?
   You shall not stir out of your house to-day.
Cæsar: Cæsar shall forth: the things that threaten'd me   10
   Ne'er look'd but on my back; when they shall see
   The face of Cæsar, they are vanished.
Calpurnia: Cæsar, I never stood on ceremonies,
   Yet now they fright me. There is one within,
   Besides the things that we have heard and seen,   15
   Recounts most horrid sights seen by the watch.
   A lioness hath whelped in the streets;
   And graves have yawn'd, and yielded up their dead;
   Fierce fiery warriors fought upon the clouds,
   In ranks and squadrons and right form of war   20
   Which drizzled blood upon the Capitol;
   The noise of battle hurtled in the air,
   Horses did neigh, an dying men did groan,
   And ghosts did shriek and squeal about the streets,
   O Cæsar! these things are beyond all use,   25

42   *without a heart:* the heart was thought to be the organ of courage; here the meaning is "cowardly"

And I do fear them.
Cæsar: What can be avoided
  Whose end is purposed by the mighty gods?
  Yet Cæsar shall go forth; for these predictions
  Are to the world in general as to Cæsar.
Calpurnia: When beggars die, there are no comets seen;   30
  The heavens themselves blaze forth the death of princes.
Cæsar: Cowards die many times before their deaths;
  The valiant never taste of death but once.
  Of all the wonders that I yet have heard,
  It seems to me most strange that men should fear;   35
  Seeing that death, a necessary end,
  Will come when it will come.

[*Re-enter Servant.*]

                    What say the augurers?
Servant: They would not have you to stir forth to-day.
  Plucking the entrails of an offering forth,
  They could not find a heart within the beast.   40
Cæsar: The gods do this in shame of cowardice:
  Cæsar should be a beast without a heart,
  If he should stay at home to-day for fear.
  No, Cæsar shall not: danger knows full well
  That Cæsar is more dangerous than he: 45
  We are two lions litter'd in one day,
  And I the elder and more terrible:
  And Cæsar shall go forth.
Calpurnia: Alas, my lord,
  Your wisdom is consumed in confidence.
  Do not go forth to-day: call it my fear   50
  That keeps you in the house, and not your own.
  We'll send Mark Antony to the senate-house;
  And he shall say you are not well to-day:
  Let me, upon my knee, prevail in this.
Cæsar: Mark Antony shall say I am not well;   55
  And for thy humour, I will stay at home.

[*Enter Decius.*]

  Here's Decius Brutus, he shall tell them so.
Decius: Cæsar, all hail! good morrow, worthy Cæsar:

60   *happy time:* just the right moment

89   *tinctures:* coats of arms. This refers to the custom of dipping handkerchiefs in the blood of martyrs to preserve a memorial of them; *stains:* the colours used in a coat of arms or family crest; *relics:* objects of reverence; *cognizance:* distinguishing badge of service

96-97   *a mock . . . render'd:* likely to be misinterpreted and laughed at

I come to fetch you to the senate-house.

Cæsar: And you are come in very happy time,   60
  To bear my greeting to the senators
  And tell them that I will not come to-day:
  Cannot, is false, and that I dare not, falser:
  I will not come to-day: tell them so, Decius.

Calpurnia: Say he is sick.

Cæsar: Shall Cæsar send a lie?   65
  Have I in conquest stretch'd mine arm so far,
  To be afeard to tell greybeards the truth?
  Decius, go tell them Cæsar will not come.

Decius: Most mighty Cæsar, let me know some cause,
  Lest I be laugh'd at when I tell them so.   70

Cæsar: The cause is in my will: I will not come;
  That is enough to satisfy the senate.
  But for your private satisfaction,
  Because I love you, I will let you know.
  Calpurnia here, my wife, stays me at home: 75
  She dreamt to-night she saw my statue,
  Which, like a fountain with an hundred spouts,
  Did run pure blood; and many lusty Romans
  Came smiling, and did bathe their hands in it:
  And these does she apply for warnings, and portents,   80
  And evils imminent: and on her knee
  Hath begg'd that I will stay at home to-day.

Decius: This dream is all amiss interpreted;
  It was a vision fair and fortunate:
  Your statue spouting blood in many pipes,   85
  In which so many smiling Romans bathed,
  Signifies that from you great Rome shall suck
  Reviving blood, and that great men shall press
  For tinctures, stains, relics, and cognizance.
  This by Calpurnia's dream is signified.   90

Cæsar: And this way have you well expounded it.

Decius: I have, when you have heard what I can say:
  And know it now: the senate have concluded
  To give this day a crown to mighty Cæsar.
  If you shall send them word you will not come,   95
  Their minds may change. Besides, it were a mock
  Apt to be render'd, for some one to say

103   *proceeding:* advancement of your career

112   *enemy:* Caesar had pardoned Caius Ligarius for having sup-
       ported Pompey

113   *ague:* disease or sickness

129   *yearns:* grieves

"Break up the senate till another time,
When Cæsar's wife shall meet with better dreams."
If Cæsar hide himself, shall they not whisper,   100
"Lo, Cæsar is afraid"?
Pardon me, Cæsar; for my dear, dear love
To your proceeding bids me tell you this,
And reason to my love is liable.
Cæsar: How foolish do your fears seem now, Calpurnia!   105
I am ashamed I did yield to them.
Give me my robe, for I will go.

[*Enter Publius, Brutus, Ligarius, Metellus, Casca, Trebonius,
and Cinna.*]

And look where Publius is come to fetch me.
Publius: Good morrow, Cæsar.
Cæsar: Welcome, Publius.
What, Brutus, are you stirr'd so early too?   110
Good morrow, Casca, Caius Ligarius,
Cæsar was ne'er so much your enemy
As that same ague which hath made you lean.
What is't o'clock?
Brutus: Cæsar, 'tis strucken eight.
Cæsar: I thank you for your pains and courtesy.   115

[*Enter Antony.*]

See! Antony, that revels long o'nights,
Is notwithstanding up. Good morrow, Antony.
Antony: So to most noble Cæsar.
Cæsar: Bid them prepare within:
I am to blame to be thus waited for.
Now, Cinna: now, Metellus: what, Trebonius!   120
I have an hour's talk in store for you;
Remember that you call on me to-day:
Be near me, that I may remember you.
Trebonius: Cæsar, I will: [*Aside*] and so near will I be,
That your best friends shall wish I had been further.   125
Cæsar: Good friends, go in, and taste some wine with me;
And we, like friends, will straightway go together.
Brutus [*Aside*]: That every like is not the same, O Cæsar,
The heart of Brutus yearns to think upon!   [*Exeunt.*]

Act 2, Scene 2: Activities

1. So far in the play we have seen Caesar as:
   • a great military hero.
   • a political leader and ruler of people.
   • a friend and husband.
   • a man, subject to the same fears and doubts most people share.

   In groups, consider one of the above aspects of Caesar's life. Find and record evidence from this scene that demonstrates this aspect of his character. Share your findings with others.

2. If you could enter this scene and warn Caesar about the real intention of the conspirators, what would you tell him?
   • How would you explain the real meaning behind the seemingly friendly words and actions of the conspirators?
   • How would you present your information so that Caesar would listen to you and believe you?

   Role play your speech to Caesar for other members of your group. Before you present your advice to Caesar be sure you explain to your audience the point in the scene where you would make the speech.

3. In this scene we are given more evidence of unnatural events ("horrid sights seen by the watch") and see the different interpretations of them made by Calpurnia, the Soothsayer, Caesar, and Decius.

   How might these unnatural events be explained by today's scientists? How would you explain them to a classmate? Share your ideas with others. You might record your feelings about unnatural events as a personal journal entry or deliver an oral report on this subject to the class.

4. In the twentieth century there have been assassinations of famous leaders such as John Kennedy, Martin Luther

King and Indira Gandhi. Choose an assassinated leader
you know about and research events that happened just
before his or her death. You might consider the following
questions as you do your research:
- Were there people who saw the leader as a threat to
  their well-being?
- Did the leader have any warnings about impending
  danger? If not, speculate about how the person might
  have felt and responded to warning signals.
- What was the effect of the assassination on the leader's
  people?

Prepare a written, oral, or visual account of your findings
when you have completed this activity.

For the next scenes . . .

If you were Caesar, would you have rejected the warnings
against going to the Capitol? Explain your response.

Act 2, Scenes 3 and 4

In these scenes . . .

While Caesar and his escorts are setting out from his house, we meet Artemidorus standing on a street that Caesar will use en route to the Capitol. Artemidorus is reading a letter that could save Caesar's life. He plans to hand Caesar the letter as Caesar passes by.

In another part of the street we see Portia, who now seems aware of what the conspirators, led by her husband, plan to do. She orders the servant Lucius to run to the senate house and bring back news of what is happening. The Soothsayer passes Portia on his way to the Capitol and states his intention to tell Caesar again about his fears of what may happen on the Ides of March.

7   *security:* overconfidence

9   *lover:* dear friend

13   *emulation:* attempt to equal or excel

15   *contrive:* conspire

Scene 3

The same. A street near the Capitol.

Enter Artemidorus, reading a paper.

Artemidorus: Cæsar, beware of Brutus; take heed of Cassius;
come not near Casca; have an eye to Cinna; trust not
Trebonius; mark well Metellus Cimber: Decius Brutus
loves thee not: thou hast wronged Caius Ligarius.
There is but one mind in all these men, and it is bent   5
against Cæsar. If thou beest not immortal, look about
you; security gives way to conspiracy. The mighty gods
defend thee!

> Thy lover, *Artemidorus.*

Here will I stand till Cæsar pass along,   10
And as a suitor will I give him this.
My heart laments that virtue cannot live
Out of the teeth of emulation.
If thou read this, O Cæsar, thou mayst live;
If not, the Fates with traitors do contrive.   [*Exit.*] 15

6   *constancy:* self-control, strength

9   *counsel:* secret

18   *rumour:* confused noise; *fray:* battle

20   *Sooth:* truly

Scene 4

*Another part of the same street,
before the house of Brutus.*

Enter Portia and Lucius.

Portia: I prithee, boy, run to the senate-house;
    Stay not to answer me, but get thee gone:
    Why dost thou stay?
Lucius: To know my errand, madam.
Portia: I would have had thee there, and here again,
    Ere I can tell thee what thou shouldst do there.   5
    O constancy, be strong upon my side!
    Set a huge mountain 'tween my heart and tongue!
    I have a man's mind, but a woman's might.
    How hard it is for women to keep counsel!
    Art thou here yet?
Lucius: Madam, what should I do?   10
    Run to the Capitol, and nothing else?
    And so return to you, and nothing else?
Portia: Yes, bring me word, boy, if thy lord look well,
    For he went sickly forth: and take good note
    What Cæsar doth, what suitors press to him.   15
    Hark, boy! what noise is that?
Lucius: I hear none, madam.
Portia: Prithee, listen well;
    I heard a bustling rumour, like a fray,
    And the wind brings it from the Capitol.
Lucius: Sooth, madam, I hear nothing.   20

    [*Enter the Soothsayer.*]

Portia: Come hither, fellow: which way hast thou been?
Soothsayer: At mine own house, good lady.
Portia: What is't o'clock?
Soothsayer: About the ninth hour, lady.
Portia: Is Cæsar yet gone to the Capitol?

27   *suit:* important message or matter of concern

37   *void:* empty

42-43   *Brutus . . . grant:* Portia makes up an excuse for her anxiety in case Lucius has overheard her.

44   *commend:* give my love

45   *merry:* cheerful

Soothsayer: Madam, not yet: I go to take my stand,   25
  To see him pass on to the Capitol.
Portia: Thou hast some suit to Cæsar, hast thou not?
Soothsayer: That I have, lady: if it will please Cæsar
  To be so good to Cæsar as to hear me,
  I shall beseech him to befriend himself.   30
Portia: Why, know'st thou any harm's intended towards
  him?
Soothsayer: None that I know will be, much that I fear
  may chance.
  Good morrow to you. Here the street is narrow:
  The throng that follows Cæsar at the heels,
  Of senators, of prætors, common suitors,   35
  Will crowd a feeble man almost to death:
  I'll get me to a place more void, and there
  Speak to great Cæsar as he comes along.   *[Exit.]*
Portia: I must go in. Ay me, how weak a thing
  The heart of woman is! O Brutus,   40
  The heavens speed thee in thine enterprise!
  Sure, the boy heard me. Brutus hath a suit
  That Cæsar will not grant. O, I grow faint.
  Run, Lucius, and commend me to my lord;
  Say I am merry: come to me again,   45
  And bring me word what he doth say to thee.
                            [Exeunt severally.]

Act 2, Scenes 3 and 4: Activities

1. Prepare a list of about three questions you would like
   to ask Artemidorus after he has read his letter to Caesar.
   Phrase your questions so they will force him to reveal
   as much about himself as possible.

   Conduct an interview, having one person be the character
   and another person use your questions as the basis for
   the interview. The success of the interview will depend
   on the quality of the answers your questions draw from
   the character.

2. After examining Portia's behaviour in Scene 4, in your
   group discuss qualities of her personality that you
   find particularly admirable and/or particularly disturbing.
   Create a profile of Portia in your journal based on these
   impressions. Have your impressions of Portia changed
   from the ones you had in Act 2, Scene 1? Add your
   response to this question in your journal entry.

3. Prepare and present a staging of one part of Scene
   4 for other members of the class. You might select
   the segment from
   • lines 1 – 20
   • lines 21 – 46, or
   • a segment of your own choosing.

   Decide how you can most effectively convey the
   emotions shown by Portia, Lucius, and the Soothsayer. Discuss your presentation with the class.

Act 2: Consider the Whole Act

1. Imagine that a friend returns to school after missing the study of Act Two. You want to give him or her information about what has happened since the end of Act One. What dialogue and action highlights would you include in your update?

2. In your journal, respond to two or three of the following statements:
   - The character I would really like to meet is . . . because . . . .
   - What I really don't understand in this act is . . . .
   - I would like to know more about what motivated . . . (a character) to . . . .
   - I have changed my mind about . . . (a character) because . . . .
   - I like/dislike scene . . . in this act because . . . .

3. With the assistance of your teacher or librarian, locate books with illustrations of ancient Roman settings. Select one or more pictures that might be appropriate for a section of a scene in this act. Using details from the picture(s), draw or write about the setting. Present your result to your group. You might make a collection of your settings for a class viewing.

4. In Act 2, we observe the wives of both Brutus and Caesar expressing concern for their husbands' safety and well-being. Today, the spouses of many political leaders play important roles in the leaders' public lives.

   Choose one partnership you know in which the spouse plays an active role in the political figure's public life.

   Prepare a set of questions you would ask the spouse if you could interview him or her for a radio or television program. Phrase the questions so that they will require the person being interviewed to reveal as much of his or her personality as possible.

5. Choose three segments from this act that you found particularly interesting and effective. With a partner, share the choices you made, explaining why you made each choice.

6. *Make a video*

   This activity is done in pairs or small groups. Select a part of a scene in this act in which you focus on the difficulty the two characters have accepting what each other is saying. Working in pairs or small groups, use the camera to create a mood.

   Rehearse the speeches a few times to be sure you are clear about the meaning of the lines, and about the words, the movement, and the interaction.

   Prepare a shooting script or storyboard in which you do the following:
   • Consider the distance between the camera and the subject that would be appropriate for each shot.
   • Determine the kind of lighting you think will best convey the mood you are seeking to create.
   • Provide one shot per complete thought.

   Have other members of the class judge how successful you have been in conveying mood through your video presentation.

For the next scene . . .

Have you ever ignored the advice of others to do something your way? What happened? What would have happened if you had followed the advice given?

What are some possible ways the disastrous events of the Ides of March might have been prevented?

Act 3, Scene 1

In this scene . . .

Ignoring the attempts of the soothsayer and Artemidorus to warn him, Caesar proceeds to the Capitol and begins to deal with the business of the senate. The conspirators attack and, at the thrust of Brutus' sword, the mighty Caesar falls dead at the base of Pompey's statue.

In a great outburst, the conspirators cry out, "liberty, freedom." The other senators and people at the Capitol become confused and fearful. Brutus attempts to gain their confidence and assume control.

The conspirators bathe their hands in Caesar's blood and set forth to explain their deed to the people of Rome. They are interrupted by the arrival of Antony's servant who has come to assure his master's safety. Brutus says that Antony shall not be harmed.

Antony enters and mourns the fallen Caesar. Brutus and Cassius confirm their promises to protect him and Brutus grants him permission to speak at Caesar's funeral. Brutus, Cassius, and the other conspirators leave.

Alone on stage Antony now reveals his true plan.

Soon, another servant arrives. He announces that Octavius Caesar is near Rome. Antony warns that Rome is still too dangerous to enter and that Octavius should wait until after the funeral for more news. Together, the servant and Antony depart carrying Caesar's body to the public marketplace.

3 *schedule:* scroll or paper

18 *makes:* makes his way

Act 3, Scene 1

*Rome. Before the Capitol; the
Senate sitting above.*

*A crowd of people; among them
Artemidorus and the Soothsayer.
Flourish. Enter Cæsar, Brutus,
Cassius, Casca, Decius, Metellus,
Trebonius, Cinna, Antony,
Lepidus, Popilius, Publius,
and others.*

Cæsar [To the Soothsayer]: The Ides of March are come.
Soothsayer: Ay, Cæsar; but not gone.
Artemidorus: Hail, Cæsar! read this schedule.
Decius: Trebonius doth desire you to o'er-read,
　At your best leisure, this his humble suit. 5
Artemidorus: O Cæsar, read mine first; for mine's a suit
　That touches Cæsar nearer: read it, great Cæsar.
Cæsar: What touches us ourself shall be last served.
Artemidorus: Delay not, Cæsar; read it instantly.
Cæsar: What, is the fellow mad?
Publius:　　　　　　　　　Sirrah, give place. 10
Cassius: What, urge you your petitions in the street?
　Come to the Capitol.
　　　[Cæsar goes up to the Senate-House, the rest following.]
Popilius: I wish your enterprise to-day may thrive.
Cassius: What enterprise, Popilius?
Popilius:　　　　　　　　　Fare you well.
　　　　　　　　　[Advances to Cæsar.]
Brutus: What said Popilius Lena? 15
Cassius: He wish'd to-day our enterprise might thrive.
　I fear our purpose is discovered.
Brutus: Look, how he makes to Cæsar: mark him.
Cassius: Casca, be sudden, for we fear prevention.

21   *turn back:* return alive

25   *knows his time:* is acting according to the plan

28   *presently prefer:* immediately present
29   *address'd:* present

33   *puissant:* powerful

36   *couchings . . . courtesies:* bowings and bending low

38-39   *turn . . . children:* make long established laws and customs like
        rules for children's games

39-42   *Be not . . . fools:* Do not be foolish enough to think that Caesar's
        spirit can be convinced to rebel against his true
        nature by that which persuades fools.

51   *repealing:* recalling

54   *freedom of repeal:* liberation from exile

Brutus, what shall be done? If this be known,   20
Cassius or Cæsar never shall turn back,
For I will slay myself.
Brutus: Cassius, be constant:
Popilius Lena speaks not of our purposes;
For, look, he smiles, and Cæsar doth not change.
Cassius: Trebonius knows his time; for, look you, Brutus, 25
He draws Mark Antony out of the way.
        [Exeunt Antony and Trebonius.]
Decius: Where is Metellus Cimber? Let him go,
And presently prefer his suit to Cæsar.
Brutus: He is address'd: press near and second him.
Cinna: Casca, you are the first that rears your hand. 30
Cæsar: Are we all ready? What is now amiss
That Cæsar and his senate must redress?
Metellus: Most high, most mighty, and most puissant Cæsar,
Metellus Cimber throws before thy seat
An humble heart:—   *[Kneeling.]*
Cæsar: I must prevent thee, Cimber. 35
These couchings and these lowly courtesies
Might fire the blood of ordinary men,
And turn pre-ordinance and first decree
Into the law of children. Be not fond,
To think that Cæsar bears such rebel blood   40
That will be thaw'd from the true quality
With that which melteth fools; I mean, sweet words,
Low-crooked court'sies and base spaniel-fawning.
Thy brother by decree is banished:
If thou dost bend and pray and fawn for him, 45
I spurn thee like a cur out of my way.
Know, Cæsar doth not wrong nor without cause
Will he be satisfied.
Metellus: Is there no voice more worthy than my own,
To sound more sweetly in great Cæsar's ear, 50
For the repealing of my banish'd brother?
Brutus: I kiss thy hand, but not in flattery, Cæsar;
Desiring thee that Publius Cimber may
Have an immediate freedom of repeal.
Cæsar: What, Brutus!
Cassius: Pardon, Cæsar; Cæsar, pardon; 55

57   *enfranchisement:* freedom

67   *apprehensive:* capable of reasoning, understanding

69   *holds on his rank:* keeps his position

74   *Olympus:* In Greek mythology this was a mountain in Greece
        where the gods lived.

75   *bootless:* in vain

80   *common pulpits:* platform for public speakers in the Forum

87   *confounded:* overwhelmed

89   *standing:* organizing a resistance or opposition

As low as to thy foot doth Cassius fall,
To beg enfranchisement for Publius Cimber.
Cæsar: I would be well moved, if I were as you;
 If I could pray to move, prayers would move me:
 But I am constant as the northern star,   60
 Of whose true-fix'd and resting quality
 There is no fellow in the firmament.
 The skies are painted with unnumber'd sparks;
 They are all fire and every one doth shine;
 But there's but one in all doth hold his place: 65
 So in the world; 'tis furnish'd well with men,
 And men are flesh and blood, and apprehensive;
 Yet in the number I do know but one
 That unassailable holds on his rank,
 Unshaked of motion: and that I am he,   70
 Let me a little show it, even in this;
 That I was constant Cimber should be banish'd,
 And constant do remain to keep him so.
Cinna: O Cæsar,——
Cæsar: Hence! wilt thou lift up Olympus?
Decius: Great Cæsar,——
Cæsar: Doth not Brutus bootless kneel?   75
Casca: Speak, hands, for me!
 [*Casca first, then the other Conspirators, and last Marcus
    Brutus stab Cæsar.*]
Cæsar: Et tu, Brute! Then fall, Cæsar!   [*Dies.*]
Cinna: Liberty! Freedom! Tyranny is dead!
 Run hence, proclaim, cry it about the streets.
Cassius: Some to the common pulpits, and cry out   80
 "Liberty, freedom, and enfranchisement!"
Brutus: People, and senators, be not affrighted;
 Fly not; stand still: ambition's debt is paid.
Casca: Go to the pulpit, Brutus.
Decius: And Cassius too.   85
Brutus: Where's Publius?
Cinna: Here, quite confounded with this mutiny.
Metellus: Stand fast together, lest some friend of Cæsar's
 should chance——
Brutus: Talk not of standing. Publius, good cheer;
 There is no harm intended to your person,   90

94   *abide:* suffer the consequences of

104   *abridged:* shortened

115   *Pompey's basis:* the base of the statue of Pompey

120   *grace his heels:* honour him by following on his heels

Nor to no Roman else: so tell them, Publius.
Cassius: And leave us, Publius; lest that the people,
  Rushing on us, should do your age some mischief.
Brutus: Do so: and let no man abide this deed,
  But we the doers.

  [*Re-enter Trebonius.*]

Cassius: Where is Antony?   95
Trebonius: Fled to his house amazed:
  Men, wives and children stare, cry out and run
  As it were doomsday.
Brutus: Fates, we will know your pleasures:
  That we shall die, we know; 'tis but the time
  And drawing days out, that men stand upon.   100
Cassius: Why, he that cuts off twenty years of life
  Cuts off so many years of fearing death.
Brutus: Grant that, and then is death a benefit:
  So are we Cæsar's friends, that have abridged
  His time of fearing death. Stoop, Romans, stoop,   105
  And let us bathe our hands in Cæsar's blood
  Up to the elbows, and besmear our swords:
  Then walk we forth, even to the market-place,
  And, waving our red weapons o'er our heads,
  Let's all cry "Peace, freedom, and liberty!"   110
Cassius: Stoop then, and wash. How many ages hence
  Shall this our lofty scene be acted over
  In states unborn and accents yet unknown!
Brutus: How many times shall Cæsar bleed in sport,
  That now on Pompey's basis lies along   115
  No worthier than the dust!
Cassius: So oft as that shall be,
  So often shall the knot of us be call'd
  The men that gave their country liberty.
Decius: What, shall we forth?
Cassius: Ay, every man away:
  Brutus shall lead; and we will grace his heels   120
  With the most boldest and best hearts of Rome.

  [*Enter a Servant.*]

Brutus: Soft! who comes here? A friend of Antony's.

131   *be resolved:* be informed to his satisfaction

136   *this untrod state:* new and confusing state of affairs

146   *Falls . . . purpose:* proves to be uncomfortably correct ("to the purpose")

152   *let blood:* killed. Surgeons would let or draw blood from a patient to purge or cleanse the person of disease. *rank:* Here, rank combines three meanings: corrupted by disease (a continuation of the medical reference in "let blood"); overgrown (too powerful); and of the same position or degree as Caesar.

Servant: Thus, Brutus, did my master bid me kneel;
  Thus did Mark Antony bid me fall down;
  And, being prostrate, thus he bade me say: 125
  Brutus is noble, wise, valiant and honest;
  Cæsar was mighty, bold, royal, and loving:
  Say I love Brutus and I honour him;
  Say I fear'd Cæsar, honour'd him and loved him.
  If Brutus will vouchsafe that Antony   130
  May safely come to him, and be resolved
  How Cæsar hath deserved to lie in death,
  Mark Antony shall not love Cæsar dead
  So well as Brutus living; but will follow
  The fortunes and affairs of noble Brutus   135
  Thorough the hazards of this untrod state
  With all true faith. So says my master Antony.
Brutus: Thy master is a wise and valiant Roman;
  I never thought him worse.
  Tell him, so please him come unto this place,   140
  He shall be satisfied, and, by my honour,
  Depart untouch'd.
Servant: I'll fetch him presently.   [*Exit.*]
Brutus: I know that we shall have him well to friend.
Cassius: I wish we may: but yet have I a mind
  That fears him much; and my misgiving still   145
  Falls shrewdly to the purpose.
Brutus: But here comes Antony.

  [*Re-enter Antony.*]

                    Welcome, Mark Antony.
Antony: O mighty Cæsar! dost thou lie so low?
  Are all thy conquests, glories, triumphs, spoils,
  Shrunk to this little measure? Fare thee well.   150
  I know not, gentlemen, what you intend,
  Who else must be let blood, who else is rank:
  If I myself, there is no hour so fit
  As Cæsar's death's hour, nor no instrument
  Of half that worth as those your swords, made rich 155
  With the most noble blood of all this world.
  I do beseech ye, if you bear me hard,
  Now, whilst your purpled hands do reek and smoke,

159   *Fulfil your pleasure:* Do with me what you wish.

160   *apt:* ready

171   *As fire . . . pity:* As one fire puts out another, so did our pity for Rome drive out our pity for Caesar.

173   *have leaden points:* are harmless

174   *in strength of malice:* with the same strength as if we were enemies

175   *temper:* attitude, i.e., with the affection of brothers

178   *dignities:* honours, offices

191   *credit:* reputation

192   *conceit:* judge

Fulfil your pleasure. Live a thousand years,
I shall not find myself so apt to die: 160
No place will please me so, no mean of death,
As here by Cæsar, and by you cut off,
The choice and master spirits of this age.
Brutus: O Antony, beg not your death of us.
   Though now we must appear bloody and cruel,   165
   As, by our hands and this our present act,
   You see we do, yet see you but our hands
   And this the bleeding business they have done:
   Our hearts you see not; they are pitiful;
   And pity to the general wrong of Rome—   170
   As fire drives out fire, so pity pity—
   Hath done this deed on Cæsar. For your part,
   To you our swords have leaden points, Mark Antony:
   Our arms in strength of malice, and our hearts
   Of brothers' temper, do receive you in   175
   With all kind love, good thoughts and reverence.
Cassius: Your voice shall be as strong as any man's
   In the disposing of new dignities.
Brutus: Only be patient till we have appeased
   The multitude, beside themselves with fear,   180
   And then we will deliver you the cause,
   Why I, that did love Cæsar when I struck him,
   Have thus proceeded.
Antony: I doubt not of your wisdom.
   Let each man render me his bloody hand:
   First, Marcus Brutus, will I shake with you: 185
   Next, Caius Cassius, do I take your hand;
   Now, Decius Brutus, yours; now yours, Metellus;
   Yours, Cinna; and my valiant Casca, yours;
   Though last, not least in love, yours, good Trebonius.
   Gentlemen all,—alas, what shall I say?   190
   My credit now stands on such slippery ground,
   That one of two bad ways you must conceit me,
   Either a coward or a flatterer.
   That I did love thee, Cæsar, O, 'tis true:
   If then thy spirit look upon us now,   195
   Shall it not grieve thee dearer than thy death,
   To see thy Antony making his peace,

202   *close:* enter into an agreement

204   *bay'd, brave hart:* hunted and trapped, courageous stag

206   *Sign'd in thy spoil:* marked by your blood; *lethe:* lifeblood. In
        Greek mythology, the Lethe was the river in Hades, the under-
        world. When people drank from it, they forgot everything about
        their lives on earth.

213   *modesty:* understatement

215   *compact:* agreement

216   *prick'd:* marked, set down

228   *Produce:* bring

Shaking the bloody fingers of thy foes,
Most noble! in the presence of thy corse?
Had I as many eyes as thou hast wounds,   200
Weeping as fast as they stream forth thy blood,
It would become me better than to close
In terms of friendship with thine enemies.
Pardon me, Julius! Here wast thou bay'd, brave hart;
Here didst thou fall, and here thy hunters stand,   205
Sign'd in thy spoil, and crimson'd in thy lethe.
O world, thou wast the forest to this hart;
And this, indeed, O world, the heart of thee.
How like a deer, strucken by many princes,
Dost thou here lie!   210

Cassius: Mark Antony——
Antony: Pardon me, Caius Cassius;
The enemies of Cæsar shall say this;
Then, in a friend, it is cold modesty.
Cassius: I blame you not for praising Cæsar so;
But what compact mean you to have with us?   215
Will you be prick'd in number of our friends,
Or shall we on, and not depend on you?
Antony: Therefore I took your hands, but was indeed
Sway'd from the point, by looking down on Cæsar.
Friends am I with you all and love you all,   220
Upon this hope, that you shall give me reasons
Why and wherein Cæsar was dangerous.
Brutus: Or else were this a savage spectacle:
Our reasons are so full of good regard
That were you, Antony, the son of Cæsar,   225
You should be satisfied.
Antony: That's all I seek:
And am moreover suitor that I may
Produce his body to the market-place;
And in the pulpit, as becomes a friend,
Speak in the order of his funeral.   230
Brutus: You shall, Mark Antony.
Cassius: Brutus, a word with you.
   [*Aside to Brutus.*] You know not what you do:
      do not consent
   That Antony speak in his funeral:

238   *protest:* announce

243   *what may fall:* what might result

257   *tide of times:* course of history

264   *cumber:* burden, weigh down

269   *choked . . . deeds:* smothered by the familiarity of terrible acts
270   *ranging:* searching widely, hunting

Know you how much the people may be moved
By that which he will utter?
Brutus: By your pardon; 235
I will myself into the pulpit first,
And show the reason of our Cæsar's death:
What Antony shall speak, I will protest
He speaks by leave and by permission,
And that we are contented Cæsar shall 240
Have all true rites and lawful ceremonies.
It shall advantage more than do us wrong.
Cassius: I know not what may fall; I like it not.
Brutus: Mark Antony, here, take you Cæsar's body.
You shall not in your funeral speech blame us, 245
But speak all good you can devise of Cæsar,
And say you do't by our permission;
Else shall you not have any hand at all
About his funeral: and you shall speak
In the same pulpit whereto I am going, 250
After my speech is ended.
Antony: Be it so;
I do desire no more.
Brutus: Prepare the body then, and follow us.
                              [*Exeunt. Antony remains.*]
Antony: O, pardon me, thou bleeding piece of earth,
That I am meek and gentle with these butchers! 255
Thou art the ruins of the noblest man
That ever lived in the tide of times.
Woe to the hand that shed this costly blood!
Over thy wounds now do I prophesy,
Which, like dumb mouths, do ope their ruby lips, 260
To beg the voice and utterance of my tongue,
A curse shall light upon the limbs of men;
Domestic fury and fierce civil strife
Shall cumber all the parts of Italy;
Blood and destruction shall be so in use, 265
And dreadful objects so familiar,
That mothers shall but smile when they behold
Their infants quarter'd with the hands of war;
All pity choked with custom of fell deeds:
And Cæsar's spirit, ranging for revenge, 270

271   *Até:* the goddess of revenge

273   *Cry "Havoc":* Give the signal for mass slaughter and looting. (Only a king could give this signal to troops.)

292   *try:* test

294   *issue:* results

295   *discourse:* relate, describe

With Até by his side come hot from hell,
Shall in these confines with a monarch's voice
Cry "Havoc!" and let slip the dogs of war;
That this foul deed shall smell above the earth
With carrion men, groaning for burial.   275

[*Enter a Servant.*]

You serve Octavius Cæsar, do you not?
Servant: I do, Mark Antony.
Antony: Cæsar did write for him to come to Rome.
Servant: He did receive his letters, and is coming;
And bid me say to you by word of mouth——   280
O Cæsar!——   [*Seeing the body.*]
Antony: Thy heart is big, get thee apart and weep.
Passion, I see, is catching; for mine eyes
Seeing those beads of sorrow stand in thine,
Began to water. Is thy master coming?   285
Servant: He lies to-night within seven leagues of Rome.
Antony: Post back with speed, and tell him what hath
    chanced:
Here is a mourning Rome, a dangerous Rome,
No Rome of safety for Octavius yet;
Hie hence, and tell him so. Yet, stay awhile;   290
Thou shalt not back till I have borne this corse
Into the market-place: there shall I try,
In my oration, how the people take
The cruel issue of these bloody men;
According to the which, thou shalt discourse   295
To young Octavius of the state of things.
Lend me your hand.   [*Exeunt with Cæsar's body.*]

121

Act 3, Scene 1: Activities

1. Write down your responses to this scene. On one side of a page under the heading "Feelings," write down words and expressions that describe the emotional reactions you experienced. On the other side of the page under the heading "Observations," list the events that happened in the scene. In small groups share your results.

   a) Have a reporter from your group present a summary of your group discussion about the scene to the rest of the class.

   b) Using your original lists and any additions or changes you have made to them as a result of your discussions, write a final account of your responses by explaining to what extent both the scene's emotional content and factual matter affected you.

2. Using the information you gained about Julius Caesar in this scene, decide whether you would have wanted him as your emperor if you had lived in Rome in 44 B.C. Record your decision and your reasons for making that decision in your journal.

3. Imagine that you are a senator of Rome who was a witness to the assassination of Caesar. Write an account of this event and your reactions to it to a colleague holding government office in another Roman province.

4. Announce the death of Caesar to the world in a news report by means of satellite television communication. One member of your group should serve as a newsroom anchorman, another as an on-site reporter. Include "live" interviews in your telecast. Compare your coverage of the event with the coverage by other "networks" (other groups).

5. If you could give Brutus some personal advice as he considers Antony's request to speak at Caesar's funeral, what would you say to him?

Write a note to be delivered by a messenger to Brutus and indicate the moment in the scene at which it should arrive. Share the note with a partner.

6. Prepare three or four questions you would like to ask Marc Antony at the end of this scene. Conduct an interview in your group having one person be the character and another person use your questions as the basis for the interview.

7. Select a section of Scene 1 that you would like to perform. Plan and rehearse your production carefully. Consider the following as you undertake the project.

Step 1: *Blocking*
Decide upon appropriate stage positions for all of the major and minor characters in the scene. Where will they stand? When, where, and how will they move?

Step 2: *Rehearsing*
Put movements and lines together. Adjust stage positions and movements as well as line delivery. Work for freshness, spontaneity and dramatic impact.

Step 3: *Using effects*
Choose appropriate sound and lighting effects.

Step 4: *Presenting*
Perform your scene. Discuss with your audience their reactions.

For the next scene . . .

What are some funeral ceremonies and procedures you know about? How have some of the people who participated in these rites behaved?

What provisions exist in the event of the sudden death of the chief political leader in a) the country in which you live or b) the country from which you (your family) originate?

Act 3, Scene 2

In this scene . . .

Brutus and Cassius must now attempt to explain their actions to the people of Rome. They divide the crowd, and Cassius leaves with some of the citizens while Brutus remains on stage. He explains that his love of Rome is greater than his love for Caesar. Sudden death was the only way to liberate Rome from the threat of rule by a tyrant. He seems to succeed in convincing the people and departs, leaving Antony to conduct the funeral rites.

Marc Antony now delivers his speech. Appealing to the crowd's most basic instincts for tears, greed, and violence, he unleashes an outburst that results in civil revolt. The political and social order is destroyed. The horrors that he predicted in Scene 1 begin to take shape. The scene ends as the citizens carry Caesar's body to the burning funeral pyre. Flames from this pyre will be used not only to ignite the conspirators' houses but also to destroy the very foundations of the great Roman Empire.

11   *severally:* separately

13   *last:* the end of the speech

14   *lovers:* dear friends

17   *censure:* judge

18   *senses:* ability to understand

26   *fortunate:* successful

Scene 2

The Forum.

*Enter Brutus and Cassius, and
a throng of Citizens.*

Citizens: We will be satisfied; let us be satisfied.
Brutus: Then follow me, and give me audience, friends.
   Cassius, go you into the other street,
   And part the numbers.
   Those that will hear me speak, let 'em stay here;   5
   Those that will follow Cassius, go with him;
   And public reasons shall be rendered
   Of Cæsar's death.
First Citizen: I will hear Brutus speak.
Second Citizen: I will hear Cassius; and compare their
   reasons,   10
When severally we hear them rendered.
          [*Exit Cassius, with some of the Citizens.*
                    Brutus goes into the pulpit.]
Third Citizen: The noble Brutus is ascended: silence!
Brutus: Be patient till the last.
   Romans, countrymen, and lovers! hear me for my cause,
   and be silent, that you may hear: believe me for mine   15
   honour, and have respect to mine honour, that you
   may believe: censure me in your wisdom, and awake
   your senses, that you may the better judge. If there be
   any in this assembly, any dear friend of Cæsar's, to
   him I say, that Brutus' love to Cæsar was no less than   20
   his. If then that friend demand why Brutus rose
   against Cæsar, this is my answer: Not that I loved Cæsar
   less, but that I loved Rome more. Had you rather
   Cæsar were living and die all slaves, than that Cæsar
   were dead, to live all freemen? As Cæsar loved me,   25
   I weep for him; as he was fortunate, I rejoice at it;
   as he was valiant, I honour him: but, as he was
   ambitious, I slew him. There is tears for his love; joy

31   *bondman:* slave
32   *rude:* uncivilized

38   *question:* reason
39   *enrolled:* registered, recorded
40   *extenuated:* lessened, undervalued
41   *enforced:* exaggerated

52   *parts:* qualities

59   *grace:* honour, respect
60   *Tending to:* relating to

for his fortune; honour for his valour; and death for
his ambition. Who is here so base that would be a   30
bondman? If any, speak; for him have I offended. Who
is here so rude that would not be a Roman? If any,
speak; for him have I offended. Who is here so vile that
will not love his country? If any, speak; for him have
I offended. I pause for a reply.   35
All: None, Brutus, none.
Brutus: Then none have I offended. I have done no more
    to Cæsar than you shall do to Brutus. The question
    of his death is enrolled in the Capitol; his glory not
    extenuated, wherein he was worthy, nor his offences   40
    enforced, for which he suffered death.

   [*Enter Antony and others, with Cæsar's body.*]

Here comes his body, mourned by Mark Antony: who,
though he had no hand in his death, shall receive
the benefit of his dying, a place in the commonwealth;
as which of you shall not? With this I depart—that,   45
as I slew my best lover for the good of Rome, I have
the same dagger for myself, when it shall please my
country to need my death.
All: Live, Brutus! live, live!
First Citizen: Bring him with triumph home unto his house.   50
Second Citizen: Give him a statue with his ancestors.
Third Citizen: Let him be Cæsar.
Fourth Citizen: Cæsar's better parts
    Shall be crown'd in Brutus.
First Citizen: We'll bring him to his house with shouts and
    clamours.
Brutus: My countrymen——
Second Citizen: Peace! Silence! Brutus speaks. 55
First Citizen: Peace, ho!
Brutus: Good countrymen, let me depart alone,
    And, for my sake, stay here with Antony:
    Do grace to Cæsar's corpse, and grace his speech
    Tending to Cæsar's glories; which Mark Antony,   60
    By our permission, is allow'd to make.
    I do entreat you, not a man depart,
    Save I alone, till Antony have spoke.   [*Exit.*]

67   *beholding:* grateful, indebted

91   *ransoms:* payment made for the release of captured enemies; *general coffers:* public treasury

First Citizen: Stay, ho! and let us hear Mark Antony.
Third Citizen: Let him go up into the public chair;   65
  We'll hear him. Noble Antony, go up.
Antony: For Brutus' sake, I am beholding to you.
                                               [*Goes into the pulpit.*]
Fourth Citizen: What does he say of Brutus?
Third Citizen: He says, for Brutus' sake
  He finds himself beholding to us all.
Fourth Citizen: 'Twere best he speak no harm of Brutus
  here.   70
First Citizen: This Cæsar was a tyrant.
Third Citizen: Nay, that's certain:
  We are blest that Rome is rid of him.
Second Citizen: Peace! Let us hear what Antony can say.
Antony: You gentle Romans——
Citizens: Peace, ho! let us hear him.
Antony: Friends, Romans, countrymen, lend me your ears;   75
  I come to bury Cæsar, not to praise him.
  The evil that men do lives after them;
  The good is oft interrèd with their bones;
  So let it be with Cæsar. The noble Brutus
  Hath told you Cæsar was ambitious: 80
  If it were so, it was a grievous fault,
  And grievously hath Cæsar answer'd it.
  Here, under leave of Brutus and the rest—
  For Brutus is an honourable man;
  So are they all, all honourable men—   85
  Come I to speak in Cæsar's funeral.
  He was my friend, faithful and just to me:
  But Brutus says he was ambitious;
  And Brutus is an honourable man.
  He hath brought many captives home to Rome,   90
  Whose ransoms did the general coffers fill:
  Did this in Cæsar seem ambitious?
  When that the poor hath cried, Cæsar hath wept:
  Ambition should be made of sterner stuff:
  Yet Brutus says he was ambitious;   95
  And Brutus is an honourable man.
  You all did see that on the Lupercal
  I thrice presented him a kingly crown,

112   *Caesar . . . wrong:* Caesar has been unjustly treated.

116   *dear abide it:* pay a heavy price for it

122   *so poor:* so low in social status, so humble

123   *disposed:* inclined

132   *commons:* common people

Which he did thrice refuse: was this ambition?
Yet Brutus says he was ambitious;   100
And, sure, he is an honourable man.
I speak not to disprove what Brutus spoke,
But here I am to speak what I do know.
You all did love him once, not without cause:
What cause withholds you then to mourn for him?   105
O judgment! thou art fled to brutish beasts,
And men have lost their reason. Bear with me;
My heart is in the coffin there with Cæsar,
And I must pause till it come back to me.
First Citizen: Methinks there is much reason in his sayings. 110
Second Citizen: If thou consider rightly of the matter,
    Cæsar has had great wrong.
Third Citizen: Has he, masters?
    I fear there will a worse come in his place.
Fourth Citizen: Mark'd ye his words? He would not take
    the crown;
    Therefore 'tis certain he was not ambitious.   115
First Citizen: If it be found so, some will dear abide it.
Second Citizen: Poor soul! his eyes are red as fire with
    weeping.
Third Citizen: There's not a nobler man in Rome than
    Antony.
Fourth Citizen: Now mark him, he begins again to speak.
Antony: But yesterday the word of Cæsar might   120
    Have stood against the world; now lies he there,
    And none so poor to do him reverence.
    O masters, if I were disposed to stir
    Your hearts and minds to mutiny and rage,
    I should do Brutus wrong, and Cassius wrong,   125
    Who, you all know, are honourable men:
    I will not do them wrong; I rather choose
    To wrong the dead, to wrong myself and you,
    Than I will wrong such honourable men.
    But here's a parchment with the seal of Cæsar;   130
    I found it in his closet, 'tis his will;
    Let but the commons hear this testament—
    Which, pardon me, I do not mean to read—
    And they would go and kiss dead Cæsar's wounds

135   *napkins:* handkerchiefs

139   *issue:* children, descendants

143   *meet:* fitting

152   *o'ershot myself:* gone further than I intended

171   *mantle:* Caesar's toga

And dip their napkins in his sacred blood, 135
Yea, beg a hair of him for memory,
And, dying, mention it within their wills,
Bequeathing it as a rich legacy
Unto their issue.
Fourth Citizen: We'll hear the will: read it, Mark Antony. 140
All: The will! the will! we will hear Cæsar's will.
Antony: Have patience, gentle friends, I must not read it;
It is not meet you know how Cæsar loved you.
You are now wood, you are not stones, but men;
And, being men, hearing the will of Cæsar, 145
It will inflame you, it will make you mad:
'Tis good you know not that you are his heirs;
For, if you should, O, what would come of it!
Fourth Citizen: Read the will; we'll hear it, Antony;
You shall read us the will, Cæsar's will. 150
Antony: Will you be patient? will you stay awhile?
I have o'ershot myself to tell you of it:
I fear I wrong the honourable men
Whose daggers have stabb'd Cæsar; I do fear it.
Fourth Citizen: They were traitors: honourable men! 155
All: The will! the testament!
Second Citizen: They were villains, murderers: the will! read
the will.
Antony: You will compel me then to read the will?
Then make a ring about the corpse of Cæsar,
And let me show you him that made the will. 160
Shall I descend? and will you give me leave?
All: Come down.
Second Citizen: Descend.
[*He comes down from the pulpit.*]
Third Citizen: You shall have leave.
Fourth Citizen: A ring; stand round. 165
First Citizen: Stand from the hearse, stand from the body.
Second Citizen: Room for Antony, most noble Antony.
Antony: Nay, press not so upon me; stand far off.
Several Citizens: Stand back. Room! Bear back.
Antony: If you have tears, prepare to shed them now. 170
You all do know this mantle: I remember
The first time ever Cæsar put it on;

174   *Nervii:* the most warlike of the Gallic tribes. In 57 B.C., Caesar fought courageously and overpowered this tribe. His victory was celebrated with great rejoicing.

176   *rent:* tear

180   *to be resolved:* to be assured

182   *Caesar's angel:* close friend of Caesar's

195   *dint:* force

197   *vesture:* garment, clothing

198   *marr'd:* mangled

'Twas on a summer's evening, in his tent,
That day he overcame the Nervii:
Look, in this place ran Cassius' dagger through: 175
See what a rent the envious Casca made:
Through this the well-beloved Brutus stabb'd;
And as he pluck'd his cursed steel away,
Mark how the blood of Cæsar follow'd it,
As rushing out of doors, to be resolved   180
If Brutus so unkindly knock'd, or no;
For Brutus, as you know, was Cæsar's angel:
Judge, O you gods, how dearly Cæsar loved him!
This was the most unkindest cut of all;
For when the noble Cæsar saw him stab,   185
Ingratitude, more strong than traitors' arms,
Quite vanquish'd him: then burst his mighty heart;
And, in his mantle muffling up his face,
Even at the base of Pompey's statue,
Which all the while ran blood, great Cæsar fell.   190
O, what a fall was there, my countrymen!
Then I, and you, and all of us fell down,
Whilst bloody treason flourish'd over us.
O, now you weep, and I perceive you feel
The dint of pity: these are gracious drops.   195
Kind souls, what weep you when you but behold
Our Cæsar's vesture wounded? Look you here,
Here is himself, marr'd, as you see, with traitors.
First Citizen: O piteous spectacle!
Second Citizen: O noble Cæsar!   200
Third Citizen: O woeful day!
Fourth Citizen: O traitors, villains!
First Citizen: O most bloody sight!
Second Citizen: We will be revenged.
All: Revenge! About! Seek! Burn! Fire! Kill! Slay! Let not
  a traitor live!   205
Antony: Stay, countrymen.
First Citizen: Peace there! hear the noble Antony.
Second Citizen: We'll hear him, we'll follow him, we'll die
  with him.
Antony: Good friends, sweet friends let me not stir you up
  To such a sudden flood of mutiny.   210

212   *private griefs:* personal complaints or causes

219   *public leave:* permission to speak in public

222   *right on:* directly

227   *ruffle up:* enrage, incite to riot

248   *arbours:* gardens

They that have done this deed are honourable:
What private griefs they have, alas, I know not,
That made them do it: they are wise and honourable,
And will, no doubt, with reasons answer you.
I come not, friends, to steal away your hearts: 215
I am no orator, as Brutus is;
But, as you know me all, a plain blunt man,
That love my friend; and that they know full well
That gave me public leave to speak of him:
For I have neither wit, nor words, nor worth, 220
Action, nor utterance, nor the power of speech,
To stir men's blood: I only speak right on;
I tell you that which you yourselves do know;
Show you sweet Cæsar's wounds, poor poor dumb
    mouths,
And bid them speak for me: but were I Brutus, 225
And Brutus Antony, there were an Antony
Would ruffle up your spirits, and put a tongue
In every wound of Cæsar, that should move
The stones of Rome to rise and mutiny.
All: We'll mutiny. 230
First Citizen: We'll burn the house of Brutus.
Third Citizen: Away, then! come, seek the conspirators.
Antony: Yet hear me, countrymen; yet hear me speak.
All: Peace, ho! Hear Antony. Most noble Antony!
Antony: Why, friends, you go to do you know not what: 235
    Wherein hath Cæsar thus deserved your loves?
    Alas, you know not: I must tell you then:
    You have forgot the will I told you of.
All: Most true: the will! Let's stay and hear the will.
Antony: Here is the will, and under Cæsar's seal. 240
    To every Roman citizen he gives,
    To every several man, seventy-five drachmas.
Second Citizen: Most noble Cæsar! We'll revenge his death.
Third Citizen: O royal Cæsar!
Antony: Hear me with patience. 245
All: Peace, ho!
Antony: Moreover, he hath left you all his walks,
    His private arbours and new-planted orchards,
    On this side Tiber; he hath left them you,

254   *the holy place:* the part of the Forum where bodies were
       cremated

255   *brands:* pieces of burning wood

266   *upon a wish:* just as I had hoped; *Fortune:* the goddess of fate

And to your heirs for ever; common pleasures,　　　　250
To walk abroad and recreate yourselves.
Here was a Cæsar! when comes such another?
First Citizen: Never, never. Come, away, away!
　We'll burn his body in the holy place,
　And with the brands fire the traitors' houses.　　255
　Take up the body.
Second Citizen: Go fetch fire.
Third Citizen: Pluck down benches.
Fourth Citizen: Pluck down forms, windows, anything.
　　　　　　　　　　[Exeunt Citizens with the body.]
Antony: Now let it work. Mischief, thou art afoot,　260
　Take thou what course thou wilt!

[Enter a Servant.]

　　　　　　　　　　　How now, fellow!
Servant: Sir, Octavius is already come to Rome.
Antony: Where is he?
Servant: He and Lepidus are at Cæsar's house.
Antony: And thither will I straight to visit him:　　265
　He comes upon a wish. Fortune is merry,
　And in this mood will give us anything.
Servant: I heard him say, Brutus and Cassius
　Are rid like madmen through the gates of Rome.
Antony: Belike they had some notice of the people,　270
　How I had moved them. Bring me to Octavius.
　　　　　　　　　　　　　　[Exeunt.]

Act 3, Scene 2: Activities

1. After reading and/or listening several times to Brutus's speech and Antony's speech to the citizens, write down your responses to each one. You may wish to use the following questions to help you organize your comments:
   - For what reason does each speaker address the crowd?
   - What feelings did you experience as you read and/or heard each speech?
   - What effect does each speech have on Brutus's and Antony's audience?
   - What is there about the way each speech is written and presented that accounts for this effect? Consider elements such as the following: idea content, language, length, and audience participation.

   Discuss your written responses with others in your group. Write a summary of the group's feelings about each speech, assessing the overall effectiveness of each delivery.

2. Recall the responses of audiences at rock concerts, baseball games, and/or wrestling matches that you have seen or heard about. What characteristics of these modern-day audiences are similar to those of Antony's audience? What characteristics are different?

3. Think of a social issue about which you feel strongly (in favour of it or against it). Write down all your reasons for wanting to defend or attack the cause.
   - Prepare a speech that you could deliver to persuade your audience to believe as you do.
   - See how many of Antony's oratorical techniques you can employ in your speech.
   - Deliver your speech to other members of your class.

4. You are a Roman centurion whose job it is to control the crowd at the public funeral for Caesar. Write the report that you make to your supervisor describing the crowd

at the end of Brutus's speech and at the end of Antony's delivery. Explain what your staff did to try to control the crowd.

5. Write a speech that Cassius might have delivered to those citizens who chose to follow him "into the other street." With fellow students, present a scene in which he delivers the speech and which shows the citizens' reaction to it. Does it provoke the same reaction as did that of Brutus? Why or why not?

6. Prepare three drawings that show Antony speaking to the crowd at three different stages of his oration. Try to illustrate the ways in which Antony achieves his objectives. Share your results with others.

For the next scene . . .

Have you experienced, heard about, or read about a crowd that got out of control? What happened? How was order restored? What are some things organizers of crowd attractions and officers of the law do to prevent mob scenes? What threats to personal and public safety does senseless mob behaviour pose?

Act 3, Scene 3

In this scene . . .

Cinna the poet appears on a street near the Forum. He speaks of a threatening dream and expresses fears of what may happen to him. A band of unruly citizens arrives. They mistakenly believe that he is Cinna the conspirator. Even after they realize their mistake, they senselessly slay him and continue on a rampage of violence and destruction through the city streets.

2   *charge:* fill; *fantasy:* imaginings

18   *bear me a bang:* receive a blow from me

27   *Cinna:* Helvius Cinna, the poet. The historian Plutarch records that the rioting citizens mistook him for Cinna, the conspirator, and killed him.

Scene 3

The same. A street.

Enter Cinna the poet.

Cinna: I dreamt to-night that I did feast with Cæsar,
And things unluckily charge my fantasy:
I have no will to wander forth of doors,
Yet something leads me forth.

[*Enter Citizens.*]

First Citizen: What is your name?   5
Second Citizen: Whither are you going?
Third Citizen: Where do you dwell?
Fourth Citizen: Are you a married man or a bachelor?
Second Citizen: Answer every man directly.
First Citizen: Ay, and briefly.   10
Fourth Citizen: Ay, and wisely.
Third Citizen: Ay, and truly, you were best.
Cinna: What is my name? Whither am I going?
  Where do I dwell? Am I a married man or a bachelor?
    Then, to answer every man dircctly and briefly, wisely 15
    and truly: wisely I say, I am a bachelor.
Second Citizen: That's as much as to say, they are fools that
    marry: you'll bear me a bang for that, I fear. Proceed;
    directly.
Cinna: Directly, I am going to Cæsar's funeral.   20
First Citizen: As a friend or an enemy?
Cinna: As a friend.
Second Citizen: That matter is answered directly.
Fourth Citizen: For your dwelling, briefly.
Cinna: Briefly, I dwell by the Capitol.   25
Third Citizen: Your name, sir, truly.
Cinna: Truly, my name is Cinna.
First Citizen: Tear him to pieces; he's a conspirator.

33-34   *pluck . . . going:* Simply tear his name out of his heart and let him go.

Cinna: I am Cinna the poet, I am Cinna the poet.

Fourth Citizen: Tear him for his bad verses, tear him for   30
    his bad verses.

Cinna: I am not Cinna the conspirator.

Fourth Citizen: It is no matter, his name's Cinna; pluck but
    his name out of his heart, and turn him going.

Third Citizen: Tear him, tear him! Come brands, ho!   35
    firebrands: to Brutus', to Cassius'; burn all: some
    to Decius' house, and some to Casca's; some to
    Ligarius': away, go!   [*Exeunt.*]

Act 3, Scene 3: Activities

1. Write a newspaper feature on the attack on Cinna the poet. In your account, try to include the following:
   - how and why the crowd were provoked to attack Cinna,
   - how Cinna might have avoided the confrontation,
   - why nobody could control the crowd, and
   - how the crowd took the law in their own hands to avenge the murder of Caesar.

   In your feature story, include your opinion on crowd violence. Comment too on whether you think Marc Antony had anything to do with promoting Cinna's untimely death and whether you think Cinna deserved what happened to him.

2. In your group, rehearse this scene aloud and present it to your class. You may wish to use the lines of the text or rewrite this scene in your own words.

   For your presentation try to include lighting and sound effects to heighten the mood and atmosphere you want to create for your audience.

Act 3: Consider the Whole Act

1. If you were staging a production of *Julius Caesar*, would you consider the end of this act to be a logical place to have an intermission?

   Record your response and explanation for it in your journal.

   At the end of the play review this journal note to see whether you still agree with your choice.

2. In this act Cinna, the poet, speaks of discomforting dreams. We remember Calpurnia's dream in Act 2. Invent a dream that Antony might tell about. To help you, consult your journal entries on your impression of him and recall events of the scenes in which he participates. Write a speech for Antony in which he describes his dream to Octavius.

3. Shakespeare based incidents and some of the dialogue in *Julius Caesar* on accounts he had read of the lives of Caesar, Brutus, and Marc Antony. Sometimes he altered details such as the time sequence of events to achieve the dramatic quality of his work.

   Explore some of the historical records and accounts of the assassination of Julius Caesar on the Ides of March to discover the similarities and some of the differences between the real event in history and Shakespeare's dramatic account of the event.

   Use the assistance of your teacher(s) and/or librarian to locate information for this research project. You might consider some of the following points:
   • the real date of Caesar's triumphant return to Rome
   • the time lapse between Caesar's murder and the Battle of Phillipi
   • the timing of Portia's suicide.

   Prepare a written and/or audio-visual summary of your findings and conclusions at the end of the time period specified for this activity.

4. Brutus did not anticipate the civil war that is about to erupt. Do you think any of the other conspirators did? Prepare a news report that analyses the important events leading to the war. Include in your report answers to questions such as the following:
   - What happened?
   - Where did things go wrong? Why did they go wrong?
   - Could Civil War have been prevented?
   - What will be the outcome of the war in your opinion?

   Deliver your presentation to your group and compare your opinions with those of other commentators.

5. Study political cartoons, in newspapers and magazines, that give humorous dramatic expression to political figures and political issues of today.

   With a partner, decide which character or event from Act Three could be captured in a political cartoon. Draw or write a description of the character/situation you have chosen to portray humorously.

   If you have created a visual representation, provide an appropriate caption for it.

6. In your journal, write an entry which continues the following statements:
   - I was/was not surprised by the crowd's reaction to Brutus's speech because . . . .
   - One of the most frightening things about mob behaviour is . . . .
   - What interests me most about Marc Antony is . . . .
   - I am looking forward to meeting Octavius because . . . .
   - I would enjoy seeing this play with . . . (name a friend or relative) because . . . .

For the next scene . . .

Think of places you know where large-scale civil disobedience and social violence have occurred. Some examples from history are the French Revolution, the American Revolution, the expulsion of the British from countries such as India and South Africa. In what other places have people fought for political change? How was order restored?

Did the restoration of order end the problems that had created the disobedience and violence?

What experiences have people you know or know about had when they fought a government system?

Act 4, Scene 1

In this scene . . .

This scene takes place in Antony's house. The self-appointed group of three who now rule Rome and Italy, Antony, Octavius, and Lepidus, are concluding a meeting. As the scene begins, they are drawing up a list of names of people whom they intend to put to death. Antony sends Lepidus to Caesar's house to obtain the will so they can change its terms to suit their own purposes. As soon as Lepidus departs, Antony openly reveals his true opinion of the man.

In the closing lines of the scene, Antony reports that Brutus and Cassius are recruiting armies. Both Antony and Octavius must now make careful plans to overcome the dangers that threaten their rule.

1   *prick'd:* marked (with a pinprick on the list)

9   *cut off . . . legacies:* alter the will by reducing the bequests or eliminating some of the heirs

14   *The threefold world divided:* The Roman Empire was divided into three parts: Europe, Asia, and Africa.

17   *proscription:* condemnation to die

20   *To . . . slanderous loads:* to take away some of the suspicion (blame) from ourselves

27   *in commons:* in public pastures

Act 4, Scene 1

A house in Rome.

Antony, Octavius, and Lepidus,
seated at a table.

Antony: These many, then, shall die: their names are prick'd.
Octavius: Your brother too must die; consent you, Lepidus?
Lepidus: I do consent——
Octavius: Prick him down, Antony.
Lepidus: Upon condition Publius shall not live,
   Who is your sister's son, Mark Antony.   5
Antony: He shall not live; look, with a spot I damn him.
   But, Lepidus, go you to Cæsar's house,
   Fetch the will hither, and we shall determine
   How to cut off some charge in legacies.
Lepidus: What, shall I find you here?   10
Octavius: Or here, or at the Capitol.   *[Exit Lepidus.]*
Antony: This is a slight unmeritable man,
   Meet to be sent on errands: is it fit,
   The threefold world divided, he should stand
   One of the three to share it?
Octavius: So you thought him, 15
   And took his voice who should be prick'd to die,
   In our black sentence and proscription.
Antony: Octavius, I have seen more days than you:
   And though we lay these honours on this man,
   To ease ourselves of divers slanderous loads,   20
   He shall but bear them as the ass bears gold,
   To groan and sweat under the business,
   Either led or driven, as we point the way;
   And having brought our treasure where we will
   Then take we down his load and turn him off   25
   Like to the empty ass, to shake his ears,
   And graze in commons.

30   *appoint . . . provender:* assign him a supply of food

37   *abjects:* things that have been thrown away; *orts:* leftovers, scraps

39   *Begin his fashion:* are new to him

42   *levying powers:* raising military forces

46   *covert:* hidden

47   *surest answered:* most effectively dealt with

Octavius: You may do your will;
  But he's a tried and valiant soldier.
Antony: So is my horse, Octavius; and for that
  I do appoint him store of provender: 30
  It is a creature that I teach to fight,
  To wind, to stop, to run directly on,
  His corporal motion govern'd by my spirit.
  And, in some taste, is Lepidus but so;
  He must be taught, and train'd, and bid go forth;   35
  A barren-spirited fellow; one that feeds
  On abjects, orts, and imitations,
  Which, out of use and staled by other men,
  Begin his fashion: do not talk of him
  But as a property. And now, Octavius,   40
  Listen great things: Brutus and Cassius
  Are levying powers: we must straight make head;
  Therefore let our alliance be combined,
  Our best friends made, our means stretch'd;
  And let us presently go sit in council,   45
  How covert matters may be best disclosed,
  And open perils surest answered.
Octavius: Let us do so: for we are at the stake
  And bay'd about with many enemies;
  And some that smile have in their hearts, I fear,   50
  Millions of mischiefs.   [*Exeunt.*]

Act 4, Scene 1: Activities

1. As this scene opens, Antony, Octavius, and Lepidus are concluding a meeting which has been going on for some time.

   a) Write an account of what may have been discussed earlier in the meeting. Compare your version with those of others in your group.

   b) Prepare what could have been the agenda for the meeting and a summary of the decisions made during the meeting.

   c) Decide what you think each of the three members of the triumvirate will do at the end of the meeting.

   In your journal, make a note of your impressions of Antony, Octavius, and Lepidus from this scene.

2. Think of a political, sports, or entertainment figure who has been in the news recently over some wrongdoing (taking drugs, speeding, breaking the law in some other way).
   • How have the reporters and commentators treated this person?
   • How have his or her opponents treated the person?
   • How are the actions that Antony and Octavius take in this scene similar to those of modern-day reporters who strike out at public figures for personal misdemeanours?

   a) Write a letter to a newspaper or to a radio or television station in which you give your opinion about the way the person was treated in the press.

   b) Write a letter to Antony and Octavius telling them what you think of their actions.

3. What does Antony's plan to discard Lepidus suggest to you about the nature of political power-sharing?

What example(s) of twentieth century political organizations can you think of where one branch or section has taken an action without listening to the advisory branch of the organization?

In an organization of which you have been a member, what has happened when one member of the executive refuses to share information with the others?

Discuss your experience and observations with others. Decide what qualities you think are necessary for people to share leadership effectively.

4. As a political commentator, prepare a paper for broadcast (one or two minutes in length) in which you comment on the preparations Antony and Octavius are making to defeat the opposing forces, the challenge they face, and your sense of what it is they hope to achieve.

Present your political commentary to an audience.

For the next scene . . .

Recall a situation in which a plan or important project that you and your group undertook did not turn out as you had hoped. How did you react? How did the others react? What did you decide to do?

Act 4, Scene 2

In this scene . . .

Brutus's army has set up camp in the hills of Sardis in Asia Minor. Brutus, accompanied by his officers and his boy servant, Lucius, arrives before his tent. The news that Cassius has also arrived with his army is announced. Brutus criticizes Cassius in front of Cassius's servant, Pindarus, and again in front of his own officer, Lucilius. Cassius arrives and he and Brutus meet for the first time in several months. After a brief but tense exchange, Brutus invites Cassius into his tent to discuss privately their mutual concerns.

7   *ill officers:* bad subordinate officers

16   *familiar instances:* friendly greetings

17   *conference:* discussion

21   *enforced ceremony:* artificial or strained courtesy

23   *horses hot at hand:* spirited horses held tightly in rein

Scene 2

*Camp near Sardis. Before
Brutus' tent.*

*Drum. Enter Brutus, Lucilius,
Lucius, and Soldiers; Titinius and
Pindarus meeting them.*

Brutus: Stand, ho!
Lucilius: Give the word, ho! and stand.
Brutus: What now, Lucilius! is Cassius near?
Lucilius: He is at hand; and Pindarus is come
    To do your salutation from his master.   5
Brutus: He greets me well. Your master, Pindarus,
    In his own charge, or by ill officers,
    Hath given me some worthy cause to wish
    Things done, undone: but if he be at hand,
    I shall be satisfied.
Pindarus: I do not doubt   10
    But that my noble master will appear
    Such as he is, full of regard and honour.
Brutus: He is not doubted. A word, Lucilius,
    How he received you: let me be resolved.
Lucilius: With courtesy and with respect enough;   15
    But not with such familiar instances,
    Nor with such free and friendly conference,
    As he hath used of old.
Brutus: Thou hast described
    A hot friend cooling: ever note, Lucilius,
    When love begins to sicken and decay,   20
    It useth an enforced ceremony.
    There are no tricks in plain and simple faith;
    But hollow men, like horses hot at hand,
    Make gallant show and promise of their mettle;
    But when they should endure the bloody spur,   25

26 *fall their crests:* droop their necks; *deceitful jades:* horses that seemed energetic and spirited but that were in reality worn out

29 *the horse in general:* the cavalry

46 *enlarge your griefs:* discuss your complaints in greater detail

They fall their crests, and, like deceitful jades,
Sink in the trial. Comes his army on?
Lucilius: They mean this night in Sardis to be quarter'd;
The greater part, the horse in general,
Are come with Cassius.   [*Low march within.*]
Brutus: Hark! he is arrived.   30
March gently on to meet him.

[*Enter Cassius and his powers.*]

Cassius: Stand, ho!
Brutus: Stand, ho! Speak the word along.
First Soldier: Stand!
Second Soldier: Stand!   35
Third Soldier: Stand!
Cassius: Most noble brother, you have done me wrong.
Brutus: Judge me, you gods! wrong I mine enemies?
   And, if not so, how should I wrong a brother?
Cassius: Brutus, this sober form of yours hides wrongs;   40
   And when you do them——
Brutus: Cassius, be content;
   Speak your griefs softly: I do know you well.
   Before the eyes of both our armies here,
   Which should perceive nothing but love from us,
   Let us not wrangle: bid them move away;   45
   Then in my tent, Cassius, enlarge your griefs,
   And I will give you audience.
Cassius: Pindarus,
   Bid our commanders lead their charges off
   A little from this ground.
Brutus: Lucilius, do you the like; and let no man   50
   Come to our tent till we have done our conference.
   Lucius and Titinius guard our door.   [*Exeunt.*]

Act 4, Scene 2: Activities

1. This is the first time that we have seen Brutus and Cassius since they were forced to flee Rome. What do you think has been happening to these two leaders since their departure?

   In groups, write two or three diary entries that either Cassius or Brutus could have written in their time away from each other. One group could write the entries for Cassius, while the other group prepares Brutus's entries.

   Exchange entries and discuss your responses to them.

2. Imagine that Brutus and Cassius were not able to meet at Sardis and that Brutus had to convey in a letter the concerns and feelings he has expressed to Cassius in this scene. Write the letter that Brutus might have sent to Cassius.

3. References to animals occur frequently in literature. Recall the images of a horse that appear in both Scenes 1 and 2 of this act. What are the horses compared to in these scenes? Do you find the comparisons effective? Why or why not?

   Begin recording other references to animals that appear throughout the rest of the play.

   At the end of the play, discuss other animal references you noted and your responses to them.

For the next scene . . .

What kinds of problems or situations can develop between close friends to strain their relationship? Why does a true friendship usually survive the difficulties that may threaten it?

Act 4, Scene 3

In this scene . . .

Inside the tent Brutus and Cassius begin to quarrel.
They exchange accusations and bitter insults as
the conflict becomes more and more heated. Finally,
however, the two friends become reconciled. A poet
enters and attempts to keep the two generals from
fighting. Cassius laughs at the shallow man, but Brutus
orders him removed. After calm has been restored,
Brutus confides to Cassius that his wife Portia has killed
herself.

The two commanders, Titinius and Messala, arrive.
They report that Octavius and Antony are leading their
armies to Phillipi. Brutus suggests that he and Cassius
go forth to meet their enemies. Cassius cautions Brutus not to march but rather to wait for their enemies to
attack. Brutus overrules Cassius and decides to lead
the armies into battle, departing early in the morning.
Cassius and the others leave.

While his company sleeps, the restless Brutus reads.
From out of the darkness, the ghost of Caesar
appears to him. He announces that he shall see Brutus
at Phillipi. When the apparition has dissolved, Brutus
awakens his officers who say they have seen nothing.
Making his decision quickly, Brutus gives orders to
begin the march at once.

2   *noted:* publicly disgraced

4   *praying on his side:* speaking on his behalf, defending him

5   *slighted off:* disregarded

8   *nice:* trivial, insignificant

11   *mart . . . gold:* market official positions like merchandise

15   *honours:* gives respectability to

25   *mighty . . . honours:* the great opportunities to continue being honourable and honoured

26   *may be grasped thus:* easily acquired

Scene 3

Brutus' tent.

Enter Brutus and Cassius.

Cassius: That you have wrong'd me doth appear in this:
    You have condemn'd and noted Lucius Pella
    For taking bribes here of the Sardians;
    Wherein my letters, praying on his side,
    Because I knew the man, were slighted off.   5
Brutus: You wrong'd yourself to write in such a case.
Cassius: In such a time as this it is not meet
    That every nice offence should bear his comment.
Brutus: Let me tell you, Cassius, you yourself
    Are much condemn'd to have an itching palm;   10
    To sell and mart your offices for gold
    To undeservers.
Cassius: I an itching palm?
    You know that you are Brutus that speaks this,
    Or, by the gods, this speech were else your last.
Brutus: The name of Cassius honours this corruption.   15
    And chastisement doth therefore hide his head.
Cassius: Chastisement!
Brutus: Remember March, the Ides of March remember:
    Did not great Julius bleed for justice' sake?
    What villain touch'd his body, that did stab,   20
    And not for justice? What, shall one of us,
    That struck the foremost man of all this world
    But for supporting robbers, shall we now
    Contaminate our fingers with base bribes,
    And sell the mighty space of our large honours   25
    For so much trash as may be grasped thus?
    I had rather be a dog, and bay the moon,
    Than such a Roman.

39   *choler:* anger

44   *budge:* give in

45   *observe:* pay attention to

47   *spleen:* anger. In Shakespeare's time the spleen was thought to be the bodily source of emotions.

52   *vaunting:* boasting

58   *moved:* angered

Cassius:　　　　　　　Brutus, bay not me;
　I'll not endure it: you forget yourself,
　To hedge me in; I am a soldier, I,　　　　　　　　30
　Older in practice, abler than yourself
　To make conditions.
Brutus:　　　　　　　Go to; you are not Cassius.
Cassius: I am.
Brutus: I say you are not.
Cassius: Urge me no more, I shall forget myself;　　35
　Have mind upon your health, tempt me no further.
Brutus: Away, slight man!
Cassius: Is't possible?
Brutus:　　　　　　　Hear me, for I will speak.
　Must I give way and room to your rash choler?
　Shall I be frighted when a madman stares?　　　40
Cassius: O ye gods, ye gods! must I endure all this?
Brutus: All this! ay, more: fret till your proud heart break;
　Go show your slaves how choleric you are,
　And make your bondmen tremble. Must I budge,
　Must I observe you? Must I stand and crouch　　45
　Under your testy humour? By the gods,
　You shall digest the venom of your spleen,
　Though it do split you; for, from this day forth,
　I'll use you for my mirth, yea, for my laughter,
　When you are waspish.
Cassius:　　　　　　　Is it come to this?　　　50
Brutus: You say you are a better soldier:
　Let it appear so; make your vaunting true,
　And it shall please me well: for mine own part,
　I shall be glad to learn of noble men.
Cassius: You wrong me every way; you wrong me, Brutus;　55
　I said, an elder soldier, not a better:
　Did I say better?
Brutus:　　　　　　　If you did, I care not.
Cassius: When Cæsar lived, he durst not thus have
　　moved me.
Brutus: Peace, peace! you durst not so have tempted him.
Cassius: I durst not!　　　　　　　　　　　　60
Brutus: No.
Cassius: What, durst not tempt him!

72   *coin my heart:* sell my heart for money

75   *indirection:* dishonesty

80   *rascal counters:* worthless coins, used only for counting

84   *rived:* torn apart

95   *braved:* defied

96   *Check'd:* corrected

97   *conn'd by rote:* learned by heart

Brutus: For your life you durst not.
Cassius: Do not presume too much upon my love;
   I may do that I shall be sorry for.
Brutus: You have done that you should be sorry for.   65
   There is no terror, Cassius, in your threats;
   For I am arm'd so strong in honesty
   That they pass by me as the idle wind,
   Which I respect not. I did send to you
   For certain sums of gold, which you denied me: 70
   For I can raise no money by vile means:
   By heaven, I had rather coin my heart,
   And drop my blood for drachmas, than to wring
   From the hard hands of peasants their vile trash
   By any indirection: I did send   75
   To you for gold to pay my legions,
   Which you denied me: was that done like Cassius?
   Should I have answer'd Caius Cassius so?
   When Marcus Brutus grows so covetous,
   To lock such rascal counters from his friends,   80
   Be ready, gods, with all your thunderbolts,
   Dash him to pieces!
Cassius: I denied you not.
Brutus: You did.
Cassius: I did not: he was but a fool
   That brought my answer back. Brutus hath
      rived my heart:
   A friend should bear his friend's infirmities,   85
   But Brutus makes mine greater than they are.
Brutus: I do not, till you practise them on me.
Cassius: You love me not.
Brutus: I do not like your faults.
Cassius: A friendly eye could never see such faults.
Brutus: A flatterer's would not, though they do appear   90
   As huge as high Olympus.
Cassius: Come, Antony, and young Octavius, come,
   Revenge yourselves alone on Cassius,
   For Cassius is aweary of the world;
   Hated by one he loves; braved by his brother;   95
   Check'd like a bondman; all his faults observed,
   Set in a note-book, learn'd, and conn'd by rote,

98   *To cast into my teeth:* to throw in my face

101   *Plutus:* the god of riches

108   *dishonour shall be humour:* I shall consider your insults to me
        as a fit of bad temper or an impulse.

111   *much enforced:* struck strongly and repeatedly

To cast into my teeth. O, I could weep
My spirit from mine eyes! There is my dagger,
And here my naked breast; within, a heart   100
Dearer than Plutus' mine, richer than gold:
If that thou be'st a Roman, take it forth;
I, that denied thee gold, will give my heart:
Strike, as thou didst at Cæsar; for I know,
When thou didst hate him worst, thou lovedst him better   105
Than ever thou lovedst Cassius.
Brutus: Sheathe your dagger:
Be angry when you will, it shall have scope;
Do what you will, dishonour shall be humour.
O Cassius, you are yoked with a lamb
That carries anger as the flint bears fire,   110
Who, much enforced, shows a hasty spark
And straight is cold again.
Cassius: Hath Cassius lived
To be but mirth and laughter to his Brutus,
When grief and blood ill-temper'd vexeth him?
Brutus: When I spoke that, I was ill-temper'd too.   115
Cassius: Do you confess so much? Give me your hand.
Brutus: And my heart too.
Cassius: O Brutus!
Brutus: What's the matter?
Cassius: Have not you love enough to bear with me,
When that rash humour which my mother gave me
Makes me forgetful?
Brutus: Yes, Cassius, and from henceforth, 120
When you are over-earnest with your Brutus,
He'll think your mother chides, and leave you so.
Poet [Within]: Let me go in to see the generals;
There is some grudge between 'em; 'tis not meet
They be alone.   125
Lucilius [Within]: You shall not come to them.
Poet [Within]: Nothing but death shall stay me.

[*Enter Poet, followed by Lucilius, Titinius, and Lucius.*]

Cassius: How now! what's the matter?
Poet: For shame, you generals! what do you mean?
Love, and be friends, as two such men should be;   130

179

132   *cynic:* rude person

136   *jigging fools:* writers of foolish and meaningless verses

144   *Of your philosophy . . . use:* You are not being very philosophical
       if you give in to difficulties that only happen by chance. Brutus
       followed the philosophy of Stoicism, which held that natural
       events were not chance but the expressions of the power of
       a wise and good god. Pain and suffering were not evil but natural
       and were therefore to be endured. Happiness was not neces-
       sary; it was duty, fortitude, and self-control that were important.

145   *accidental evils:* bad luck over which people have no control

154   *fell distract:* became depressed and went out of her mind

For I have seen more years, I'm sure, than ye.
Cassius: Ha, ha! how vilely doth this cynic rhyme!
Brutus: Get you hence, sirrah; saucy fellow, hence!
Cassius: Bear with him, Brutus; 'tis his fashion.
Brutus: I'll know his humour, when he knows his time.   135
　　What should the wars do with these jigging fools?
　　Companion, hence!
Cassius: 　　　　　　Away, away, be gone!
　　　　　　　　　　　　　　　　[Exit Poet.]
Brutus: Lucilius and Titinius, bid the commanders
　　Prepare to lodge their companies to-night.
Cassius: And come yourselves, and bring Messala with you 140
　　Immediately to us. 　　*[Exeunt Lucilius and Titinius.]*
Brutus: 　　　　　　Lucius, a bowl of wine! *[Exit Lucius.]*
Cassius: I did not think you could have been so angry.
Brutus: O Cassius, I am sick of many griefs.
Cassius: Of your philosophy you make no use,
　　If you give place to accidental evils.   145
Brutus: No man bears sorrow better. Portia is dead.
Cassius: Ha! Portia!
Brutus: She is dead.
Cassius: How 'scaped I killing when I cross'd you so?
　　O insupportable and touching loss!   150
　　Upon what sickness?
Brutus: 　　　　　　Impatient of my absence,
　　And grief that young Octavius with Mark Antony
　　Have made themselves so strong: for with her death
　　That tidings came: with this she fell distract,
　　And, her attendants absent, swallow'd fire.   155
Cassius: And died so?
Brutus: 　　　　　　Even so.
Cassius: 　　　　　　　　O ye immortal gods!

[Re-enter Lucius, with wine and taper.]

Brutus: Speak no more of her. Give me a bowl of wine.
　　In this I bury all unkindness, Cassius. 　　*[Drinks.]*
Cassius: My heart is thirsty for that noble pledge.
　　Fill, Lucius, till the wine o'erswell the cup;   160
　　I cannot drink too much of Brutus' love. 　　*[Drinks.]*
　　　　　　　　　　　　　　　　[Exit Lucius.]

164   *call in question:* closely examine, carefully consider

169   *bending their expedition:* directing their movement

170   *tenour:* meaning

188   *she is dead:* Brutus has already discussed Portia's death with Cassius (line 146) and yet is apparently hearing about it here for the first time from Messala. There are two theories about this duplication. Some Shakespearean scholars believe that when Shakespeare rewrote this scene, he inserted a second version (line 146) and that both versions were left in by mistake (by Shakespeare, the editor, or the printer). Other scholars think that Shakespeare intended to include both versions and that when Brutus hears about his wife's death from Messala, he is using the opportunity to reinforce his image as a Stoic.

193   *in art:* in theory or in knowledge, if not in experience

[*Re-enter Titinius, with Messala.*]

Brutus: Come in, Titinius! Welcome, good Messala.
  Now sit we close about this taper here,
  And call in question our necessities.
Cassius: Portia, art thou gone?
Brutus: No more, I pray you.   165
  Messala, I have here received letters,
  That young Octavius and Mark Antony
  Come down upon us with a mighty power,
  Bending their expedition towards Philippi.
Messala: Myself have letters of the selfsame tenour.   170
Brutus: With what addition?
Messala: That by proscription and bills of outlawry,
  Octavius, Antony, and Lepidus,
  Have put to death an hundred senators.
Brutus: Therein our letters do not well agree;   175
  Mine speak of seventy senators that died
  By their proscriptions. Cicero being one.
Cassius: Cicero one?
Messala: Cicero is dead,
  And by that order of proscription.
  Had you your letters from your wife, my lord?   180
Brutus: No, Messala.
Messala: Nor nothing in your letters writ of her?
Brutus: Nothing, Messala.
Messala: That, methinks, is strange.
Brutus: Why ask you? hear you aught of her in yours?
Messala: No, my lord.   185
Brutus: Now, as you are a Roman, tell me true.
Messala: Then like a Roman bear the truth I tell:
  For certain she is dead, and by strange manner.
Brutus: Why, farewell Portia. We must die, Messala:
  With meditating that she must die once   190
  I have the patience to endure it now.
Messala: Even so great men great losses should endure.
Cassius: I have as much of this in art as you,
  But yet my nature could not bear it so.
Brutus: Well, to our work alive. What do you think   195
  Of marching to Philippi presently?

205   *grudged us contribution:* have been reluctant to supply us

206   *by them:* through their land

213   *tried . . . friends:* have been given all the help our allies can
        give us

227   *niggard . . . rest:* take only a short rest

Cassius: I do not think it good.
Brutus: Your reason?
Cassius: This it is:
  'Tis better that the enemy seek us:
  So shall he waste his means, weary his soldiers,
  Doing himself offence; whilst we, lying still,   200
  Are full of rest, defence, and nimbleness.
Brutus: Good reasons must of force give place to better.
  The people 'twixt Philippi and this ground
  Do stand but in a forced affection,
  For they have grudged us contribution: 205
  The enemy, marching along by them,
  By them shall make a fuller number up,
  Come on refresh'd, new added, and encouraged;
  From which advantage shall we cut him off,
  If at Philippi we do face him there,   210
  These people at our back.
Cassius: Hear me, good brother.
Brutus: Under your pardon. You must note beside,
  That we have tried the utmost of our friends,
  Our legions are brim-full, our cause is ripe:
  The enemy increaseth every day;   215
  We, at the height, are ready to decline.
  There is a tide in the affairs of men
  Which taken at the flood leads on to fortune;
  Omitted, all the voyage of their life
  Is bound in shallows and in miseries.   220
  On such a full sea are we now afloat,
  And we must take the current when it serves,
  Or lose our ventures.
Cassius: Then, with your will, go on;
  We'll along ourselves, and meet them at Philippi.
Brutus: The deep of night is crept upon our talk,   225
  And nature must obey necessity;
  Which we will niggard with a little rest.
  There is no more to say?
Cassius: No more. Good night:
  Early to-morrow will we rise and hence.
Brutus: Lucius! [*Enter Lucius.*] My gown. [*Exit Lucius.*]   230
    Farewell, good Messala:

241   *o'erwatch'd:* tired out by watching and waiting

249   *watch your pleasure:* be on guard for your orders

258   *an't:* if it

Good night, Titinius: noble, noble Cassius,
Good night, and good repose.
Cassius: O my dear brother!
This was an ill beginning of the night:
Never come such division 'tween our souls!   235
Let it not, Brutus.
Brutus: Everything is well.
Cassius: Good night, my lord.
Brutus: Good night, good brother.
Titinius, Messala: Good night, Lord Brutus.
Brutus: Farewell, every one.
                   [*Exeunt all but Brutus.*]

[*Re-enter Lucius, with the gown.*]

Give me the gown. Where is thy instrument?
Lucius: Here in the tent.
Brutus: What, thou speak'st drowsily?   240
Poor knave, I blame thee not; thou art o'erwatch'd.
Call Claudius and some other of my men;
I'll have them sleep on cushions in my tent.
Lucius: Varro and Claudius!

[*Enter Varro and Claudius.*]

Varro: Calls my lord?   245
Brutus: I pray you, sirs, lie in my tent and sleep;
It may be I shall raise you by-and-by
On business to my brother Cassius.
Varro: So please you, we will stand and watch your pleasure.
Brutus: I will not have it so: lie down, good sirs;   250
It may be I shall otherwise bethink me.
Look, Lucius, here's the book I sought for so;
I put it in the pocket of my gown.
             [*Varro and Claudius lie down.*]
Lucius: I was sure your lordship did not give it me.
Brutus: Bear with me, good boy, I am much forgetful.   255
Canst thou hold up thy heavy eyes awhile,
And touch thy instrument a strain or two?
Lucius: Ay, my lord, an't please you.
Brutus: It does, my boy:
I trouble thee too much, but thou art willing.

268   *leaden:* heavy; *mace:* a ceremonial rod or stick used as a symbol of authority when arresting a person

273   *leaf:* page

280   *to stare:* to stand on end

290   *false:* out of tune

Lucius: It is my duty, sir.   260
Brutus: I should not urge thy duty past thy might;
    I know young bloods look for a time of rest.
Lucius: I have slept, my lord, already.
Brutus: It was well done; and thou shalt sleep again;
    I will not hold thee long: if I do live,   265
    I will be good to thee.   [*Music and a song.*]
    This is a sleepy tune. O murderous slumber,
    Lay'st thou thy leaden mace upon my boy,
    That plays thee music? Gentle knave, good night;
    I will not do thee so much wrong to wake thee: 270
    If thou dost nod, thou break'st thy instrument;
    I'll take it from thee; and, good boy, good night.
    Let me see, let me see; is not the leaf turn'd down
    Where I left reading? Here it is, I think.

[*Enter the Ghost of Cæsar.*]

    How ill this taper burns! Ha! who comes here?   275
    I think it is the weakness of mine eyes
    That shapes this monstrous apparition.
    It comes upon me. Art thou anything?
    Art thou some god, some angel, or some devil,
    That makest my blood cold and my hair to stare?   280
    Speak to me what thou art.
Ghost: Thy evil spirit, Brutus.
Brutus: Why comest thou?
Ghost: To tell thee thou shalt see me at Philippi.
Brutus: Well; then I shall see thee again?
Ghost: Ay, at Philippi.   285
Brutus: Why, I will see thee at Philippi, then.
                                           [*Exit Ghost.*]
    Now I have taken heart thou vanishest:
    Ill spirit, I would hold more talk with thee.
    Boy, Lucius! Varro! Claudius! Sirs, awake! Claudius!
Lucius: The strings, my lord, are false.   290
Brutus: He thinks he still is at his instrument.
    Lucius, awake!
Lucius: My lord?
Brutus: Didst thou dream, Lucius, that thou so criedst out?
Lucius: My lord, I do not know that I did cry.   295

305   *commend me:* take my greetings to

306   *set . . . before:* advance his forces early in the morning

Brutus: Yes, that thou didst: didst thou see any thing?
Lucius: Nothing, my lord.
Brutus: Sleep again, Lucius. Sirrah Claudius!
  [*To Varro.*] Fellow thou, awake!
Varro: My lord? 300
Claudius: My lord?
Brutus: Why did you so cry out, sirs, in your sleep?
Varro, Claudius: Did we, my lord?
Brutus: Ay: saw you anything?
Varro: No, my lord, I saw nothing.
Claudius: Nor I, my lord.
Brutus: Go and commend me to my brother Cassius; 305
  Bid him set on his powers betimes before,
  And we will follow.
Varro, Claudius: It shall be done, my lord.   [*Exeunt.*]

Act 4, Scene 3: Activities

1. In this quarrel scene, the tone of argument ranges from cold fury to hot anger. Scorn and defiance are expressed, and threats are made. Eventually the two participants reassert their friendship and resume planning battle action.

   Prepare a short dialogue between two close friends in which they quarrel because one believes the other has done something dishonest. You will need to establish the following:
   • the setting for the quarrel and the circumstances around the argument
   • the actual accusations and responses made
   • the climax of the argument
   • the conclusion to the dialogue.

   Present your dialogue to your group. Discuss what your presentation illustrated about human emotions and close friendships.

   In your journal, record your feelings about experiences you have had or know about in which good friends have a heated argument.

   You might use this material later for developing a poem or short story about arguments.

2. How do you feel about Cassius and Brutus after this quarrel scene? Has your opinion of either one or both of them changed? Discuss your ideas. Add to or adjust your profiles of these characters if necessary as a result of your discussion.

3. Imagine that you are an officer in Brutus's or Cassius's army. Prepare a short speech that would answer Brutus's question, "What do you think of marching to Phillipi presently?"

Insert your speech at an appropriate place in the scene and stage the scene segment including your speech for others in the class.

4. Review the character profile you have developed for Brutus. Think of someone you know or know about who reminds you of Brutus.

   Write a description of the person. Which characteristics are similar to those of Brutus? Which ones are different?

5. Recall some ghost stories you have read and/or been told. Share one or two of them with a partner. Discuss the following questions:
   • What main effect does a ghost story have on its audience?
   • How does the appearance of Caesar's ghost create a similar effect?

6. With your group, prepare a stage presentation of the ghost scene. Consider the following:
   • What reminders of the past do you wish to suggest? What predictions about the future can you make?
   • What characteristics of Brutus do you wish to emphasize?
   • About which characteristics of Caesar do you wish to remind your audience?
   • What lighting and sound effects can you use to establish the appropriate atmosphere and create a definite mood?

   Present your scene. Observe other versions of this scene presented by other groups and discuss them. Decide what four or five qualities made the performances effective.

Act 4: Consider the Whole Act

1. Expressing your own reactions, complete two or three of the following statements in your journals.
   - I believe that Cassius has/has not changed since the first half of the play because . . . .
   - I am not surprised at Antony's attitude toward Lepidus because . . . .
   - Brutus's reaction to the news of Portia's death does/ does not surprise me because . . . .
   - I think that Antony and Octavius are/are not likely to succeed in their battle with Brutus and Cassius because . . . .

2. Make a tape recording or write a news report on the events that have occurred since the assassination of Caesar. Predict what you think will happen when the two sides go into battle at Phillipi in Macedonia.

3. Imagine that you are a friend of one of the senators whom Antony ordered eliminated. Write a letter to the senator's family describing the circumstances of this death. Describe your reaction and the reaction of some other people of Rome to his death and that of other senators like him.

4. Antony, Octavius, and Lepidus are carrying out a reign of terror in Rome. Research another time and place in history where drastic action was taken to change the existing political system.

   You could investigate an event in another century, such as the French Revolution in the eighteenth century; or, you could consider one in the twentieth century, like the Stalinist purges.

   What recent overthrows of government could you explore? Prepare a written, oral, or visual account of your findings and conclusions when you have completed your research.

5. If you were a military advisor to Brutus and wanted to suggest how he could prepare for the challenges and

difficulties that threaten him as he goes into battle, what would you say? In your group, discuss what weaknesses of character you would suggest that he try to control. What strengths of character would you urge him to employ? What other advice would you give him? Present your ideas to other groups.

OR

As a foreign correspondent, conduct an interview with Brutus outside his tent as he is about to leave for the plains of Phillipi. Write five or six questions you would ask. Phrase your questions so they will require Brutus to reveal as much as possible about his strategic plans and his doubts and fears about the success of his leadership and his armies' conquests.

6. *Make a video*

Choose a conversation between two characters in this act. Rehearse the lines with a partner. Be sure you are clear about the meaning of each sentence, the movement, and the interactions that occur.

As you prepare a shooting script, keep in mind the following:
- Consider the distance between the camera and the subject that you are shooting. Changing the distance will change the size of the subject and the balance of the shot. These changes will alter the mood.
- Determine the kind of lighting you think will best convey the mood you want to create.
- Decide on the angles you think will be most effective.
- Provide one visual shot per complete thought.
- Design an audio lead-in of appropriate music before the visual portion actually begins. The scene could be ended in the same manner.

For the next scene . . .

Imagine you and a partner are about to enter an important competition against strong opponents. What would you say to your partner just before the match?

Act 5, Scene 1

In this scene . . .

The action now moves to the plains of Phillipi where the armies of Octavius and Antony are camped. A messenger announces the arrival of their enemies, the armies of Brutus and Cassius. Octavius decides to lead his forces from the right of the field, thereby overruling Antony's directions.

Brutus and Cassius enter with their armies and engage in a verbal battle with Octavius and Antony. Octavius challenges Brutus to more active combat and withdraws his forces. While Brutus and his officer move aside to talk, Cassius confides to Messala his doubts about the threatening circumstances in which he finds himself.

Alone on stage, Brutus and Cassius consider the possible outcomes of this day. They exchange farewells and part to face the victory or defeat which lies ahead.

5   *warn:* challenge

7   *in their bosoms:* in on their secrets

16   *softly on:* steadily forward

19   *exigent:* crisis

21   *They . . . parley:* They are stopping and asking for a conference.

Act 5, Scene 1

The Plains of Philippi.

Enter Octavius, Antony, and their army.

Octavius: Now, Antony, our hopes are answered:
   You said the enemy would not come down,
   But keep the hills and upper regions;
   It proves not so: their battles are at hand;
   They mean to warn us at Philippi here,   5
   Answering before we do demand of them.
Antony: Tut, I am in their bosoms, and I know
   Wherefore they do it: they could be content
   To visit other places; and come down
   With fearful bravery, thinking by this face   10
   To fasten in our thoughts that they have courage;
   But 'tis not so.

[*Enter a Messenger.*]

Messenger: Prepare you, generals:
   The enemy comes on in gallant show;
   Their bloody sign of battle is hung out,
   And something to be done immediately.   15
Antony: Octavius, lead your battle softly on,
   Upon the left hand of the even field.
Octavius: Upon the right hand I; keep thou the left.
Antony: Why do you cross me in this exigent?
Octavius: I do not cross you; but I will do so.   [*March.*]   20

[*Drum. Enter Brutus, Cassius, and their army; Lucilius, Titinius, Messala, and others.*]

Brutus: They stand, and would have parley.
Cassius: Stand fast, Titinius: we must out and talk.
Octavius: Mark Antony, shall we give sign of battle?

33   *The posture of your blows:* your skill as a soldier

34   *Hybla:* a mountain in Sicily well known for its sweet honey

43   *cur:* a mongrel dog, a cowardly person

48   *Come . . . cause:* Get to the point.

49   *proof of it:* test to decide the argument

52   *goes up again:* is returned to its sheath

Antony: No, Cæsar, we will answer on their charge.
    Make forth; the generals would have some words.   25
Octavius: Stir not until the signal.
Brutus: Words before blows: is it so, countrymen?
Octavius: Not that we love words better, as you do.
Brutus: Good words are better than bad strokes, Octavius.
Antony: In your bad strokes, Brutus, you give good words: 30
    Witness the hole you made in Cæsar's heart,
    Crying "Long live! hail, Cæsar!"
Cassius: Antony,
    The posture of your blows are yet unknown:
    But for your words, they rob the Hybla bees,
    And leave them honeyless.
Antony: Not stingless too.   35
Brutus: O, yes, and soundless too;
    For you have stol'n their buzzing, Antony,
    And very wisely threat before you sting.
Antony: Villains, you did not so, when your vile daggers
    Hack'd one another in the sides of Cæsar: 40
    You show'd your teeth like apes, and fawn'd like hounds,
    And bow'd like bondmen, kissing Cæsar's feet;
    Whilst damned Casca, like a cur, behind
    Struck Cæsar on the neck. O you flatterers!
Cassius: Flatterers! Now, Brutus, thank yourself: 45
    This tongue had not offended so to-day,
    If Cassius might have ruled.
Octavius: Come, come, the cause: if arguing make us sweat;
    The proof of it will turn to redder drops.
    Look;   50
    I draw a sword against conspirators;
    When think you that the sword goes up again?
    Never, till Cæsar's three and thirty wounds
    Be well avenged, or till another Cæsar
    Have added slaughter to the sword of traitors.   55
Brutus: Cæsar, thou canst not die by traitors' hands,
    Unless thou bring'st them with thee.
Octavius: So I hope;
    I was not born to die on Brutus' sword.
Brutus: O, if thou wert the noblest of thy strain,
    Young man, thou couldst not die more honourable.   60

61   *peevish:* childish, pouting

66   *when you have stomachs:* when you have the courage

68   *on the hazard:* at stake

77   *Epicurus:* He was a Greek philosopher who believed that the gods were not interested in the affairs of humans and that, therefore, unnatural events were not to be taken seriously and omens were not to be trusted.

79   *presage:* foretell events

80   *former:* first, foremost

81   *fell:* swooped down

83   *consorted:* accompanied

Cassius: A peevish schoolboy, worthless of such honour,
  Join'd with a masker and a reveller!
Antony: Old Cassius still!
Octavius: Come, Antony, away!
  Defiance, traitors, hurl we in your teeth:
  If you dare fight to-day, come to the field;   65
  If not, when you have stomachs.
                [*Exeunt Octavius, Antony, and their army.*]
Cassius: Why, now, blow wind, swell billow and swim bark!
  The storm is up, and all is on the hazard.
Brutus: Ho, Lucilius! hark, a word with you.
Lucilius [*Standing forth*]:   My lord?
                [*Brutus and Lucilius converse apart.*]
Cassius: Messala!   70
Messala [*Standing forth*]: What says my general?
Cassius: Messala,
  This is my birthday; as this very day
  Was Cassius born. Give me thy hand, Messala:
  Be thou my witness that against my will,
  As Pompey was, am I compell'd to set   75
  Upon one battle all our liberties.
  You know that I held Epicurus strong
  And his opinion: now I change my mind,
  And partly credit things that do presage.
  Coming from Sardis, on our former ensign   80
  Two mighty eagles fell, and there they perch'd
  Gorging and feeding from our soldiers' hands;
  Who to Philippi here consorted us:
  This morning are they fled away and gone;
  And in their steads do ravens, crows and kites   85
  Fly o'er our heads and downward look on us,
  As we were sickly prey: their shadows seem
  A canopy most fatal, under which
  Our army lies, ready to give up the ghost.
Messala: Believe not so.
Cassius: I but believe it partly: 90
  For I am fresh of spirit and resolved
  To meet all perils very constantly.
Brutus: Even so, Lucilius.
Cassius: Now, most noble Brutus,

101   *that philosophy:* Stoicism – a reference to the Stoic belief that pain and suffering were natural to life and should be endured willingly.

102   *Cato:* a bitter opponent of Caesar who fought with Pompey. After the followers of Pompey were defeated, Cato committed suicide rather than be captured by Caesar.

107   *providence:* divine will

The gods to-day stand friendly, that we may,
Lovers in peace, lead on our days to age!   95
But since the affairs of men rest still incertain,
Let's reason with the worst that may befall.
If we do lose this battle, then is this
The very last time we shall speak together:
What are you then determined to do?   100
Brutus: Even by the rule of that philosophy
By which I did blame Cato for the death
Which he did give himself; I know not how,
But I do find it cowardly and vile,
For fear of what might fall, so to prevent   105
The time of life: arming myself with patience
To stay the providence of some high powers
That govern us below.
Cassius: Then, if we lose this battle,
You are contented to be led in triumph
Thorough the streets of Rome?   110
Brutus: No, Cassius, no: think not, thou noble Roman,
That ever Brutus will go bound to Rome:
He bears too great a mind. But this same day
Must end that work the Ides of March begun;
And whether we shall meet again I know not.   115
Therefore our everlasting farewell take:
For ever and for ever, farewell, Cassius!
If we do meet again, why, we shall smile;
If not, why then this parting was well made.
Cassius: For ever and for ever, farewell, Brutus!   120
If we do meet again, we'll smile indeed;
If not, 'tis true this parting was well made.
Brutus: Why, then, lead on. O, that a man might know
The end of this day's business ere it come!
But it sufficeth that the day will end,   125
And then the end is known. Come, ho! away!
                                          [*Exeunt.*]

Act 5, Scene 1: Activities

1. How would you describe Octavius's personality from what you have observed in this scene? What are his strengths of character? What are his weaknesses? Do you think Octavius has the makings of an effective leader? Share your opinions with a partner? You could make a note of your opinions in your journal. Refer to these notes and adjust them if necessary as you read through the rest of this act.

2. Flashbacks are used in films and television productions to show what happened earlier in the story. As a director filming this scene, you choose to include flashbacks during the argument that occurs between the two sets of enemies.

   a) In your group, decide on two situations from earlier in the play that you would use as flashbacks and decide where you would insert them during the argument.

   b) Compare your flashbacks and the places you inserted them with the ones other groups have selected.

3. In your journal, record your feelings towards Cassius as he bids farewell to Brutus at the end of this scene. If you have been developing a profile of Cassius, notice how this entry compares with ones you made earlier. How is it the same? different? Share your observations with others.

4. In Act 1, Scene 2, Cassius talks to Brutus about the possibility of conspiring against Caesar (lines 90–177). Contrast the mood and action of this exchange between the two men with the farewell scene between them in this scene (lines 93–126). With a partner, improvise both of these scene segments to show the differences in the mood of each.

   Have your audience identify the contrasts in moods and explain them in their own words.

5. In a movie or a story, the ending is usually the logical outcome of situations and events that occur earlier. In this scene, there are several clues about future events.

   Select lines from this scene that provide these clues. With a partner, discuss your choices and explain why you think Shakespeare provides the audience with this guiding information.

For the next scenes . . .

Recall a situation you experienced or know about in which one or more people totally misinterpreted the evidence in front of them. What happened?

Act 5, Scenes 2 and 3

In these scenes . . .

Brutus crosses the battlefield, giving orders for his wing to attack the soldiers of Octavius.

A tired and defeated Cassius arrives in another part of the field. He believes that all is lost. With the help of his servant Pindarus, he commits suicide, dying upon the same sword with which he stabbed Caesar.

Titinius, who was sent by Cassius to appraise the field, returns with the news that Brutus has defeated Octavius. He has arrived too late, however. He discovers the dead Cassius and, in the Roman tradition of showing respect and loyalty toward his leader, Titinius kills himself. Brutus enters and, grieving, he pays tribute to Cassius and Titinius. He then orders his armies to a second battle.

1   *bills:* written orders

4   *but cold demeanour:* no enthusiastic desire to fight

5   *push:* attack

Scene 2

The same. The field of battle.

Alarum. Enter Brutus and Messala.

Brutus: Ride, ride, Messala, ride and give these bills
    Unto the legions on the other side.   *[Loud alarum.]*
    Let them set on at once; for I perceive
    But cold demeanour in Octavius' wing,
    And sudden push gives them the overthrow.   5
    Ride, ride, Messala; let them all come down.
                                [Exeunt.]

1 *villains:* Cassius is referring to his own troops.

2 *mine own:* my own soldiers

3 *ensign:* flag-bearer

7 *fell to spoil:* began looting

21 *thick:* weak, nearsighted

Scene 3

Another part of the field.

*Alarums. Enter Cassius and
Titinius.*

Cassius: O, look, Titinius, look, the villains fly!
  Myself have to mine own turn'd enemy:
  This ensign here of mine was turning back;
  I slew the coward, and did take it from him.
Titinius: O Cassius, Brutus gave the word too early: 5
  Who, having some advantage on Octavius,
  Took it too eagerly: his soldiers fell to spoil,
  Whilst we by Antony are all enclosed.

  [*Enter Pindarus.*]

Pindarus: Fly further off, my lord, fly further off;
  Mark Antony is in your tents, my lord: 10
  Fly, therefore, noble Cassius, fly far off.
Cassius: This hill is far enough. Look, look, Titinius;
  Are those my tents where I perceive the fire?
Titinius: They are, my lord.
Cassius: Titinius, if thou lovest me,
  Mount thou my horse and hide thy spurs in him,   15
  Till he have brought thee up to yonder troops
  And here again; that I may rest assured
  Whether yond troops are friend or enemy.
Titinius: I will be here again, even with a thought.
                                             [*Exit.*]

Cassius: Go, Pindarus, get higher on that hill;   20
  My sight was ever thick; regard Titinius,
  And tell me what thou notest about the field.
                          [*Pindarus ascends the hill.*]
  This day I breathed first: time is come round,
  And where I did begin, there shall I end;
  My life is run his compass. Sirrah, what news?   25
Pindarus [*Above*]: O my lord!

31   *lights:* dismounts (from his horse)

43   *hilts:* handle of the sword

48   *Durst . . . will:* if I had dared to do as I wished

Cassius: What news?

Pindarus [*Above*]: Titinius is enclosed round about
  With horsemen, that make to him on the spur;
  Yet he spurs on. Now they are almost on him.   30
  Now, Titinius! Now some light. O, he lights too.
  He's ta'en. [*Shout.*] And, hark! they shout for joy.

Cassius: Come down, behold no more.
  O coward that I am, to live so long,
  To see my best friend ta'en before my face!   35

                                    [*Pindarus descends.*]

  Come hither, sirrah:
  In Parthia did I take thee prisoner;
  And then I swore thee, saving of thy life,
  That whatsoever I did bid thee do,
  Thou shouldst attempt it. Come now, keep thine oath;   40
  Now be a freeman: and with this good sword,
  That ran through Cæsar's bowels, search this bosom.
  Stand not to answer: here, take thou the hilts;
  And when my face is cover'd, as 'tis now,
  Guide thou the sword. [*Pindarus stabs him.*] Cæsar, thou
    art revenged,   45
  Even with the sword that kill'd thee.   [*Dies.*]

Pindarus: So, I am free; yet would not so have been,
  Durst I have done my will. O Cassius!
  Far from this country Pindarus shall run,
  Where never Roman shall take note of him.   [*Exit.*]   50

  [*Re-enter Titinius with Messala.*]

Messala: It is but change, Titinius; for Octavius
  Is overthrown by noble Brutus' power,
  As Cassius' legions are by Antony.

Titinius: These tidings will well comfort Cassius.

Messala: Where did you leave him?

Titinius: All disconsolate,   55
  With Pindarus his bondman, on this hill.

Messala: Is not that he that lies upon the ground?

Titinius: He lies not like the living. O my heart!

Messala: Is not that he?

Titinius: No, this was he, Messala,
  But Cassius is no more. O setting sun,   60

67   *O . . . child:* What terrible mistakes and misunderstandings are
      caused by depression and desperation.

68   *apt thoughts:* easily impressed or influenced

84   *misconstrued:* misunderstood

87   *apace:* quickly

89   *Roman's part:* It was considered an honourable act to show
      one's loyalty to a friend or superior officer by dying with him
      for the same cause.

As in thy red rays thou dost sink to night,
So in his red blood Cassius' day is set;
The sun of Rome is set. Our day is gone;
Clouds, dews, and dangers come; our deeds are done!
Mistrust of my success hath done this deed.   65
Messala: Mistrust of good success hath done this deed.
O hateful error, melancholy's child,
Why dost thou show to the apt thoughts of men
The things that are not? O error, soon conceived,
Thou never comest unto a happy birth,   70
But kill'st the mother than engender'd thee!
Titinius: What, Pindarus! where art thou, Pindarus?
Messala: Seek him, Titinius, whilst I go to meet
The noble Brutus, thrusting this report
Into his ears: I may say, thrusting it;   75
For piercing steel and darts envenomed
Shall be as welcome to the ears of Brutus
As tidings of this sight.
Titinius: Hie you, Messala,
And I will seek for Pindarus the while.
                              [*Exit Messala.*]
Why didst thou send me forth, brave Cassius?   80
Did I not meet thy friends? and did not they
Put on my brows this wreath of victory,
And bid me give it thee? Didst thou not hear their shouts?
Alas, thou hast misconstrued every thing!
But, hold thee, take this garland on thy brow;   85
Thy Brutus bid me give it thee, and I
Will do his bidding. Brutus, come apace,
And see how I regarded Caius Cassius.
By your leave, gods: this is a Roman's part:
Come Cassius' sword, and find Titinius' heart.
                              [*Kills himself.*] 90

[*Alarum. Re-enter Messala, with Brutus, young Cato, and
    Lucilius and others.*]

Brutus: Where, where, Messala, doth his body lie?
Messala: Lo, yonder, and Titinius mourning it.
Brutus: Titinius' face is upward.
Cato: He is slain.

101   *fellow:* equal

104   *Thasos:* an island in the Aegean Sea near Phillipi

Brutus: O Julius Cæsar, thou art mighty yet!
    Thy spirit walks abroad, and turns our swords   95
    In our own proper entrails.   [*Low alarums.*]
Cato: Brave Titinius!
    Look whether he have not crown'd dead Cassius!
Brutus: Are yet two Romans living such as these?
    The last of all the Romans, fare thee well!
    It is impossible that ever Rome   100
    Should breed thy fellow. Friends, I owe moe tears
    To this dead man than you shall see me pay.
    I shall find time, Cassius, I shall find time.
    Come therefore, and to Thasos send his body:
    His funerals shall not be in our camp,   105
    Lest it discomfort us. Lucilius, come;
    And come, young Cato; let us to the field.
    Labeo and Flavius, set our battles on.
    'Tis three o'clock; and, Romans, yet ere night
    We shall try fortune in a second fight.   [*Exeunt.*] 110

Act 5, Scenes 2 and 3: Activities

1. Write an obituary for Cassius as it might appear today in a newspaper or news magazine.

2. What were Cassius's reasons for committing suicide? If you had been with Cassius just before he took his life, what might you have said to him? What did he say earlier in the play that seems to contradict his decision to have Pindarus kill him?

3. Cassius followed the philosophy of Stoicism. With the assistance of your teacher and/or librarian, find out how followers of Stoicism viewed suicide. How would you adjust your comments to Cassius from activity 2 to allow for his belief in Stoicism? What would you add or say differently?

4. Pindarus takes Cassius's sword and kills Cassius at his own request. Titinius, on seeing the dead body of Cassius, takes his own life. What do the actions of these two men suggest about the relationship between Roman leaders and their officers and servants?

   With your group, discuss the relationships you have observed between officers and leaders in war movies you have seen or heard about. How do they compare with those between Cassius and his men?

   If Cassius were fighting in a battle today, what would you expect would happen if he asked one of his officers to kill him? How might the officer respond?

5. If you were one of Brutus's officers, what advice would you give him about his military position at present? What plan of attack would you recommend he follow for his "second fight"? You may wish to do some research on battles of ancient Roman times before answering this question.

Present the results of your research and your military counsel to Brutus in an oral report to classmates. You could include diagrams, maps, and charts to illustrate your military planning.

For the next scenes . . .

What qualities in a person's character can help him or her to continue in a competitive struggle even when winning seems unlikely?

Act 5, Scenes 4 and 5

In these scenes . . .

The battle continues as Brutus, in hand to hand combat, kills young Cato, one of Antony's soldiers. Soon, Lucilius, one of Brutus's most important officers, is captured. It is apparent that Octavius and Antony are emerging as the winners.

Brutus appears with the remnants of his weary army. In spite of his officers' attempts to encourage him, Brutus is convinced that all is lost, that his enemies have won. At the sound of the enemies' approach, he bids his soldiers farewell and orders them to flee to a safer spot. He and his servant, Strato, stay. He gives Strato his sword and orders him to hold it forward. Brutus ends his life by running upon the sword.

The victors arrive. Seeing the fallen Brutus before him, Antony praises Brutus as "the noblest Roman of them all," and Octavius, Caesar's successor, delivers a final tribute. He proclaims the battle ended, promises a soldier's funeral with all honours for Brutus, and departs from the field to share in the glories of his victory.

12   *Only . . . die:* I will surrender only if you will kill me.

Scene 4

Another part of the field.

*Alarum. Enter fighting, Soldiers of
both armies; among them Brutus,
young Cato, and Lucilius.*

Brutus: Yet, countrymen, O yet hold up your heads!
Cato: What bastard doth not? Who will go with me?
  I will proclaim my name about the field.
  I am the son of Marcus Cato, ho!
  A foe to tyrants, and my country's friend;   5
  I am the son of Marcus Cato, ho!
Brutus: And I am Brutus, Marcus Brutus, I;
  Brutus, my country's friend; know me for Brutus!
                        [Exit. Cato falls.]
Lucilius: O young and noble Cato, art thou down?
  Why, now thou diest as bravely as Titinius;   10
  And mayst be honour'd, being Cato's son.
First Soldier: Yield, or thou diest.
Lucilius: Only I yield to die;
  There is so much that thou wilt kill me straight;
                        [Offering money.]
  Kill Brutus, and be honour'd in his death.
First Soldier: We must not. A noble prisoner!   15
Second Soldier: Room, ho! Tell Antony, Brutus is ta'en.
First Soldier: I'll tell the news. Here comes the general.

  [Enter Antony.]

  Brutus is ta'en, Brutus is ta'en, my lord.
Antony: Where is he?
Lucilius: Safe, Antony; Brutus is safe enough: 20
  I dare assure thee that no enemy
  Shall ever take alive the noble Brutus:

32   *is chanced:* has turned out

The gods defend him from so great a shame!
When you do find him, or alive or dead,
He will be found like Brutus, like himself.   25
Antony: This is not Brutus, friend; but, I assure you,
    A prize no less in worth: keep this man safe;
    Give him all kindness: I had rather have
    Such men my friends than enemies. Go on,
    And see whether Brutus be alive or dead;   30
    And bring us word unto Octavius' tent
    How everything is chanced.   [*Exeunt.*]

2   *show'd the torch-light:* (Statilius) went to Cassius's camp to see
if it had been captured by the enemy and held up his torch
to indicate that all was well there.

15   *list:* listen

18   *several:* separate

Scene 5

Another part of the field.

Enter Brutus, Dardanius, Clitus,
Strato, and Volumnius.

Brutus: Come, poor remains of friends, rest on this rock.
Clitus: Statilius show'd the torch-light, but, my lord,
　He came not back: he is or ta'en or slain.
Brutus: Sit thee down, Clitus: slaying is the word;
　It is a deed in fashion. Hark thee, Clitus. 　　　　　　5
　　　　　　　　　　　　　　　　[*Whispering.*]
Clitus: What, I, my lord? No, not for all the world.
Brutus: Peace then, no words.
Clitus: 　　　　　　　　I'll rather kill myself.
Brutus: Hark thee, Dardanius. 　　　　[*Whispering.*]
Dardanius: 　　　　　　　Shall I do such a deed?
Clitus: O Dardanius!
Dardanius: O Clitus! 　　　　　　　　　　　　10
Clitus: What ill request did Brutus make to thee?
Dardanius: To kill him, Clitus. Look, he meditates.
Clitus: Now is that noble vessel full of grief,
　That it runs over even at his eyes.
Brutus: Come hither, good Volumnius; list a word. 　　15
Volumnius: What says my lord:
Brutus: 　　　　　　　　Why this, Volumnius:
　The ghost of Cæsar hath appear'd to me
　Two several times by night; at Sardis once,
　And this last night here in Philippi fields:
　I know my hour is come.
Volumnius: 　　　　　　　Not so, my lord. 　　20
Brutus: Nay, I am sure it is, Volumnius.
　Thou seest the world, Volumnius, how it goes;
　Our enemies have beat us to the pit: 　　[*Low alarums.*]
　It is more worthy to leap in ourselves,
　Than tarry till they push us. Good Volumnius, 　　25

46   *smatch:* touch, taste

Thou know'st that we two went to school together:
Even for that our love of old, I prithee,
Hold thou my sword-hilts, whilst I run on it.
Volumnius: That's not an office for a friend, my lord.

           [*Alarum still.*]

Clitus: Fly, fly, my lord; there is no tarrying here.   30
Brutus: Farewell to you; and you; and you, Volumnius.
 Strato, thou hast been all this while asleep;
 Farewell to thee too, Strato. Countrymen,
 My heart doth joy that yet in all my life
 I found no man but he was true to me.   35
 I shall have glory by this losing day,
 More than Octavius and Mark Antony
 By this vile conquest shall attain unto.
 So, fare you well at once; for Brutus' tongue
 Hath almost ended his life's history: 40
 Night hangs upon mine eyes; my bones would rest,
 That have but labour'd to attain this hour.

    [*Alarum. Cry within:* "Fly, fly, fly!"]

Clitus: Fly, my lord, fly!
Brutus: Hence! I will follow.

   [*Exeunt Clitus, Dardanius, and Volumnius.*]

 I prithee, Strato, stay thou by thy lord:
 Thou art a fellow of a good respect;   45
 Thy life hath had some smatch of honour in it:
 Hold then my sword, and turn away thy face,
 While I do run upon it. Wilt thou, Strato?
Strato: Give me your hand first. Fare you well, my lord.
Brutus: Farewell, good Strato. [*Runs on his sword.*] Cæsar,
 now be still: 50
 I kill'd not thee with half so good a will.   [*Dies.*]

[*Alarum. Retreat. Enter Octavius, Antony, Messala, Lucilius,
 and the Army.*]

Octavius: What man is that?
Messala: My master's man. Strato, where is thy master?
Strato: Free from the bondage you are in, Messala:
 The conquerors can but make a fire of him;   55
 For Brutus only overcame himself,
 And no man else hath honour by his death.

60   *entertain:* take into my service

61   *bestow thy time with me:* spend your life in my service

62   *prefer:* recommend

76   *use:* treat

79   *Most . . . honourably:* give full military honours

81   *part:* divide

Lucilius: So Brutus should be found. I thank thee, Brutus,
That thou has proved Lucilius' saying true.
Octavius: All that served Brutus, I will entertain them. 60
Fellow, wilt thou bestow thy time with me?
Strato: Ay, if Messala will prefer me to you.
Octavius: Do so, good Messala.
Messala: How died my master, Strato:
Strato: I held the sword, and he did run on it. 65
Messala: Octavius, then take him to follow thee,
That did the latest service to my master.
Antony: This was the noblest Roman of them all:
All the conspirators, save only he,
Did that they did in envy of great Cæsar; 70
He only, in a general honest thought
And common good to all, made one of them.
His life was gentle, and the elements
So mix'd in him that Nature might stand up
And say to all the world "This was a man!" 75
Octavius: According to his virtue let us use him,
With all respect and rites of burial.
Within my tent his bones to-night shall lie,
Most like a soldier, order'd honourably.
So call the field to rest; and let's away, 80
To part the glories of this happy day.
                              [*Exeunt omnes.*]

Act 5, Scenes 4 and 5: Activities

1. Recall an effective large-scale battle scene you have viewed in a movie. How did the director involve the audience in the action of the battle? What techniques did the director use to convey both the physical and emotional realities of the fight scene?

   Does film have an advantage over the stage for depicting a major battle scene? Explain your answer.

   How does Shakespeare keep his audience aware of the battle that takes place throughout much of this act? How does he create a sense of both the physical and emotional aspects of battle?

2. Record a final entry about Brutus in your journal. What happens in these scenes to confirm and/or deepen your understanding of this man?

3. Look back in this act to the last words Cassius said to Pindarus before he died (Scene 3, lines 33–46) and the ones that Brutus said to his officers and servant (Scene 5, lines 31–42). Why is each speech effective as a final farewell?

   How are their speeches similar? In what ways does each speech confirm or add to your understanding of each of these leading characters? Which of the two men would you have preferred as a best friend? Why?

4. Write a speech that could be part of a funeral oration delivered by Antony at Brutus's funeral. Include some of the feelings that Antony expresses in his final speech of the play. Record your speech on tape or on paper and share it with others.

5. As a group activity, present Scene(s) 4 and/or 5 to the class. You may decide to use the lines of the text or to rewrite the scene(s) in modern dialogue.

Discuss your presentation with your audience. The success of it may be judged by the audience's understanding of the message(s) you were attempting to convey.

6. With your group, write a newspaper article or prepare a news report for radio or television on the final events in the play. In your article or report:
   • bring your audience up to date on the final outcome of the political and military conflict that has been occurring.
   • include street interviews with some of the citizens of Rome and the soldiers who are returning from the wars.
   • make some final predictions about Octavius's chances of restoring law and order to the Roman Empire.

   Present your article or report to your class. Compare your account with those of other groups. Discuss similarities and differences in the various presentations.

Consider the Whole Play

1. Review the actions of both Brutus and Antony in this play. List the problems that Brutus faced on one side of the page and note the actions he took to deal with them on the other side of the page. Do the same with Antony Could either one have changed the course of events by acting differently? Explain your answer. Share your responses with others in your group or class.

2. Write a political commentary of the play as it might appear in a newspaper or magazine you know. You might include topics such as:
   • social violence
   • loyalty and trust between friends
   • ambitious leaders and blind followers
   • defeat and victory
   • state control.

3. Identify a social or political issue that is a concern in your community, country, or another part of the world. Select a character from the play *Julius Caesar* whose experiences might have included elements related to the issue. With a partner, interview the character. Ask questions that would require the character to explain how he or she would handle the problem. Record the conversation and share it with an audience.

4. At the end of the play, Octavius begins his career as a political leader. From what you have observed about him, make some predictions about what you think he might have accomplished during his reign. After you have listed your ideas, investigate some reference materials on his life and his rule. Compare your findings with your predictions. Share your discoveries with others.

5. Look back at the cover illustration for this play. What central idea or theme in *Julius Caesar* do you think the picture communicates? Now that you have read the play, choose another major theme that could have been used for the illustration. With a partner, create rough illustrations for one or more themes from *Julius Caesar*. In your group, decide which sketch you think is most effective and complete the final illustration. Display your illustrations with ones from other groups for an audience.

6. a) Review the illustrations that appear throughout this text. With your group, discuss your responses to some of these visual representations, including your comments about the following:
   • what the scenes describe
   • what feelings you have as you study the illustrations and what aspect(s) of the illustrations prompt those feelings
   • what value the illustrations have for the text of a play
   • what other illustrations might have been included.

b) With the assistance of members of the Art Department, locate one or more students who could work along with you in creating your own illustration for one or more of the scenes. Before you begin, resolve questions such as the following:
- What moment from the scene will you depict in your illustration?
- What character(s) and background detail will you include?
- What emotion do you want your viewer to feel as he or she studies the illustration? How will you convey that emotion?

7. There are many examples in history of military figures who became powerful political leaders. With the help of your librarian or teacher, select one of these military figures and prepare a written profile on the individual. Compare the personality and career of this person with that of Julius Caesar.

8. a) Review all of your journal entries on Brutus. On a sheet of paper, draw up two columns under the headings "Strengths" and "Weaknesses." In the appropriate column, list what you consider to be important qualities of Brutus's character.

   b) Write a profile summary of Brutus, explaining the following:
   - ways in which his strengths contributed to his successes
   - ways in which his weaknesses contributed to his failures
   - those qualities of his character which brought about events that arouse feelings of pity and regret in audience members
   - those aspects of his character that remind audiences of their own human strengths and weaknesses.

   Discuss your ideas and first draft of your paper with your teacher and others in your group before preparing your final version.

9. Imagine you are an actor. You have just been given the role of one of the play's important characters. Write a letter to a close friend telling him or her the good news. In your letter explain to your friend:
   - what role you will be playing
   - what there is about this character that will both challenge and excite you as an actor
   - how you intend to prepare for the part
   - what aspects of the character's personality you would like to highlight in your interpretation
   - ways in which you feel you could communicate your understanding of the character to an audience
   - other feelings or ideas you have about this opportunity.

   As you prepare this activity, you may choose to discuss the way in which an actor prepares a part with a student studying drama in college or with a member of your community who has had experience working in theatre.

10. Imagine that a touring production of *Julius Caesar* is coming to your community. You want to encourage people to attend a performance. Prepare a slide show of events from the play which will attract an audience. Use members of your class to stage the events appropriate to your purpose. Photograph each of these incidents on slides. Write a monologue to connect the incidents. Choose appropriate background music for your slides so that the whole presentation makes an emotional impact. Present your slide show to an audience.

11. You are a director. Select a part of a scene that you particularly like and do the following:
   - Decide what you think its main idea is.
   - Discuss with the actors who will play the scene how they will speak the lines and how they will present the action.
   - Create a prompt book in which you make notes to yourself about such decisions as stage directions, pauses, points of emphasis, and lighting and sound cues.

Direct the scene using this prompt book. After suitable rehearsal time, present the scene to the class. Follow the performance with a discussion between performers and audience in which the participants evaluate the presentation.

12. *Make a video*
Prepare a portion of a scene for a video production that you think could create a strong emotional impact on an audience. Consider the following questions before you make your video:
- Who will deliver the lines and present the actions?
- What emotion do you wish to focus on? How will you achieve the effect of the emotion?
- What camera angles will you use for each frame of your segment: close-up, medium close-up, or distanced?
- How many shots will you use?
- What lighting effects might help to create the appropriate atmosphere?
- What music and other sound effects will you use?

Show the complete video to your class.

13. Shakespeare wrote all of his plays for performance upon a stage. Four centuries after they were written they are still playing to audiences in theatres everywhere in the world. In the twentieth century they have often been adapted for film and video presentation.

What do you think are some of the advantages of seeing a staged production of *Julius Caesar* rather than a filmed version? What advantages does a filmed presentation offer?

Present your opinions with those of others in your group in a panel discussion for the class. Before you make your presentation, consider the following points:
- One student should be appointed as a leader to set time limits for each speaker and guide the discussion to keep it moving.

- Each panel member should present his or her opinions and respond to those of others.
- The leader could then invite members of the audience to ask questions and express opinions.
- At the end of the presentation, the leader should summarize points that have been made and conclude the event.

The panel discussion could be presented live or could be taped for later showing.

14. With the help of your teacher or a librarian, investigate other plays by William Shakespeare or those of other playwrights. Imagine that you have been asked to suggest two or three for later study. In a letter to your teacher, suggest your choices and explain why you think they would be interesting plays for students to experience.